T0304669

NEVER TRUST A LOCAL

INSIDE THE NIXON WHITE HOUSE

NEVER TRUST A LOCAL

Inside the Nixon White House

Charles Stuart

Algora Publishing
New York

Library of Congress Cataloging-in-Publication Data —

Stuart, Charles E. (Charles Edward), 1937-
Never trust a local: inside the Nixon White House / by Charles E. Stuart.
    p. cm.
    ISBN 0-87586-398-1 (trade paper: alk. paper) — ISBN 0-87586-399-X (hard
cover: alk. paper) 0-87586-400-7 — ISBN 0-87586-400-7 (ebook)
    1. Presidents—United States—Election—1968—Anecdotes. 2. Nixon,
Richard M. (Richard Milhous), 1913—Anecdotes. 3. Nixon, Richard M.
(Richard Milhous), 1913—Friends and associates—Anecdotes. 4. Stuart,
Charles E. (Charles Edward), 1937—Anecdotes. 5. Political campaigns—
United States—History—20th century—Anecdotes. 6. United States—Politics
and government—1963-1969—Anecdotes. 7. United States—Politics and
government—1969-1974—Anecdotes. I. Title.

    E851.S84 2005
    324.973'0924—dc22
                            2005013095

Front Cover: "Sock it to me" was an expression on a popular TV show of the
time. Signs like this one in Bangkok, Thailand, don't just appear. They are
ordered up by advance men, in this case, Dan Kingsley.

Printed in the United States

To my friend
Edward L. Morgan
1938-2002

TABLE OF CONTENTS

NOTE TO READERS

Many times over the past 30 years, since I left the White House staff, I have been asked if I was going to write a book. My answer has always been "no." Books by veterans of presidential administrations are written by senior level staff, which I was not, or they are expected to divulge racy secrets, of which I have none. Moreover, I believe it would be disloyal to tell tales regarding the Nixons. I have no desire to be remembered in that context. Enough of the former Nixon staff has already donned that dubious mantle.

But, watching the agony and excitement of the 2004 campaign between Bush and Kerry, I was reminded of how little new there is in presidential politics. Of course, there has been some change. We didn't have "red and blue" states in 1968. The entire budget for the Nixon campaign, the most expensive up to that time, was a little over $30 million. And, of course, there were no "527" organizations, Internet, cable news channels, or cell phones. Other things have not changed.

This, then, is a collection of the little stories, the incidents, the anecdotes that contribute to the drama of a campaign. These are small items, some serious, some humorous, but none likely to be addressed in the writings of more famous authors. Richard Nixon's memoirs did not include such inconsequential — yet, illustrative — issues. As there seems to be considerable interest in the White House and how it operates, I have shared some views from Pennsylvania Avenue, and with these come my opinions on several White House personalities.

Charles E. Stuart
Rose Hill Farm
Port Tobacco, Md.
August 2005

ACKNOWLEDGEMENTS

First, I must recognize Maj. General Craig Hagan, USA (Ret.) and Carolyne "Putzen" Krause, high school classmates. We were sitting in Putzen's kitchen with her husband John, drinking coffee and spinning yarns, when she burst out — "Charlie, you should write a book." The fact is, I had already been thinking about it. Putzen pushed me over the edge.

I wish to thank a White House associate, speech writer and author William Safire, for providing inspiration. I have long admired both his intellect and facility with words. During the production of this work, I frequently found myself thinking, "how would Safire say this?"

I appreciate the efforts of my neighbor, Jack Warren, who read my first draft and suggested improvements. Jack is a published historian and a scholar on American presidents. Reviewing this modest effort must have seemed like an undeserved punishment.

For helping me in my research, I thank Susan Nolte of the Nixon Library, Joseph Eagan of the Enoch Pratt Free Library, Diane Johnson of the Charles County Library, Maria Downs of the White House Historical Association and Pat Anderson, Sam Rushay, Michael J. Hamilton, Stephen H. Green and Allen W. Rice of the National Archives.

Helen Thomas of Hearst Publications, formerly of UPI, read an early draft and urged me to continue. As she has written two best sellers in her long career covering the White House, I was encouraged.

A friend, Kate Zabriskie, helped me with photo-editing and I thank her.

I thank my wife, Connie, for her patience and editing skills as she helped me refine the manuscript.

Finally, I wish to recognize my father, deceased since 1995. He taught me to read and to write and to appreciate the English language.

1. Making the Team

Since my previous visits to Miami had been in the winter, I was unprepared for the heat of August. I would have thought that Republicans could have found a cooler place to hold their 1968 national convention, particularly one that promised to generate some heat of its own. Still, I couldn't complain. I was on my vacation, working as a volunteer, and I was thrilled to be there.

I was assigned to John Nidecker's group, a small team responsible for the generation of excitement in and around the convention hall itself. Nidecker's nickname was "Rally John." I learned that he was a legendary Nixon advance man, having worked in that capacity in Nixon campaigns since 1952. He was a much older man than the rest of us "30 somethings," probably 50 at the time, totally bald, on the smallish side, but quite trim and indefatigable. He was a middle level manager with the Cities Service Corporation. They were apparently happy to let him participate in Nixon election campaigns whenever they occurred. Rally John gave me my first taste of operating at a responsible level in a presidential political race. I found I liked the flavor.

It was our job to create the balloon drops and balloon rises in the hall, the signs, the music, the spontaneous demonstrations and the crowds outside the hall when the convention was in session. Nixon needed 667 votes to win the nomination over the other two candidates, Governors Reagan and Rockefeller. One of the team members created a large back-lighted sign that flashed "667"; it would be on stage, ready to be switched on when the magic number was reached.

The rules did not permit any signs on the convention building or grounds but directly across the street from the main entrance to the convention center was a high-rise building on the face of which a Rockefeller operative had hung a huge banner saying, "ROCKEFELLER CAN WIN." Every delegate saw this message as he went into the center, and it aggravated Rally John to no end. I thought I might find a way to nullify its effect by putting a Nixon sign above it. I contacted the building owner and asked him if he would lease us space over the Rockefeller sign. "No," he wouldn't. Rockefeller's people had leased the whole face of the building for the week. Undeterred, I went to the building next door and, for a substantial fee, leased the roof.

I had two more problems: time, and wind. The local sign companies, already burdened with various convention orders, couldn't produce a large painted sign in time. Further, a painted banner or solid sign on the roof would be subject to wind loading and we couldn't very well have a Nixon sign blow off and possibly injure people. As I thought about the problem, I recognized that the signs that are towed by airplanes had to be large enough to be read by people on the ground. They also had to be fairly porous so as to be unaffected by the wind. Most importantly, they had to be easily made up.

I engaged an aerial advertising company to create a sign that stated, "NIXON WILL WIN," using the kind of four-foot high letters that were normally stuck on netting and towed behind planes. I then got a carpentry contractor to construct a wooden frame on the roof and we hung the sign from the frame. Next, I hired a searchlight truck and got permission from the city of Miami to have it parked on the edge of the convention grounds. The Nixon sign over shadowed the Rockefeller banner, as it was: bigger, more positive, and brightly lit. Finally, I rented a powerful public address system. I put this and a group of eye-catching Nixonettes on the roof, singing the campaign song "Nixon's the One" and leading cheers. The effect was overwhelming. Nixon owned the neighborhood.

At the end of the convention Nixon held a small celebration for about 75 people at the Key Biscayne Hotel. Since I was not high enough in the hierarchy to have been invited, Rally John took me along. Nixon played the piano and joked with people in the crowd. He was at the top of his game and was very excited, as were we all. Although I had been working for the man for months, this was the first time I had been up close in a room with him. It was an exhilarating, heady experience. Campaign fever, a highly contagious disease, infected me.

It is strange how small accomplishments sometimes turn out to be important. My creativity with the sign brought me to the attention of John Ehrlichman, who asked me to join his team of advance men. That would mean taking a leave of absence from my job with the Walter E. Heller Company in New York City; I told him I would discuss it with my employer and my wife and let him know the day after I got back to New York.

I had also been asked by Jim Skidmore, the Vice Chairman of Citizens for Nixon, to be the field director for the New England region at a salary rate of $25,000 a year — more than my salary with Heller. However, I felt the unpaid advance man job to be a much more interesting position, with the chance to be around Nixon, Bob Haldeman, Ehrlichman and the senior campaign staff. Connie, my wife, agreed that it was an opportunity too good to pass up. The Heller Company put me on half pay for the campaign (no longer legal under the present campaign finance regulations). I called John Ehrlichman and said yes.

Every school child knows the little story attributed to Benjamin Franklin: "For the want of a nail, the shoe was lost. For the want of a shoe, the horse was lost. For the want of a horse, the rider was lost. For the want of a rider, the battle was lost. For the want of the battle, the kingdom was lost. And all for the want of a nail." It graphically illustrates the impact of even the smallest of actions on the largest of events. And it was little thing like that which made the difference in getting me to Florida as a Nixon volunteer in the first place.

In the mid-1960s, a friend named Dick Whitney, who also became an advance man, had introduced me to Bill Kilgallon, who invited me to join Manhattan's Ohio Society. This was an organization whose principal reason for existence seemed to be to provide an excuse for young people from the Buckeye State to get together and party. I signed up, mostly to meet girls. Kilgallon's father was the owner of the Ohio Art Company, manufacturers of the popular toy *Etch a Sketch*. He was also a long-time financial backer of Richard M. Nixon. Both Dick and Bill were volunteers, working part time for the Nixon Campaign. I asked them if there was anything I could do to assist. I was a lifelong Republican from a Republican family, admired Richard Nixon, and wanted to help him get elected.

In late 1967 Bill asked me if I wanted to help out with a telephone solicitation effort set up by Maurice Stans, who was President Eisenhower's Director of the Bureau of the Budget and later the Secretary of Commerce in the first Nixon Administration. The effort was directed at "fat cats," a group of wealthy contributors who had donated generously to Nixon in earlier campaigns. This was before any of the 1968 primaries and Nixon, having lost his last two campaigns for elective office, was viewed as a dark horse candidate, a very dark horse.

Raising money for what appeared, to many pundits, a lost cause was expected to be difficult. Nonetheless, if the campaign were to mount a first-rate effort in New Hampshire and other early primary states, it had to have seed money. Somewhere, money had to be found in order to give Nixon a chance to prove himself as a real candidate.

I went to the headquarters building one or two nights a week and called people, some of whom were icons in American business. I tried to talk them into joining the fray, once again, by contributing to a Nixon campaign. These people were smart and tough. They hadn't gotten rich by donating to every telephone solicitation. Moreover, we were not calling for chump change, but real money.

I must have done a fairly good job with my work on the telephone, for in the spring of 1968 I got a call at my office from Jim Skidmore, a recent past president of the national Jaycee organization and current head of field operations for the Citizens for Nixon campaign. Skidmore asked me to come to Washington to meet with him and discuss how I might be of greater help in getting Nixon elected.

As I was to learn, there were two separate but parallel campaign organizations: the Nixon for President Committee based in New York City and the Citizens for Nixon group in Washington, DC. The Nixon for President group ran the actual campaign for the Presidency while the Citizens organized the grass roots support. Both groups were working to win a good showing in the primaries. The Citizens were also engaged in trying to capture delegates to the Republican convention who would support Nixon.

In Washington I visited Jim Skidmore in the old Willard Hotel, a building in a state of advanced disrepair that had been leased to the Nixon organization after having been closed for some years. (The Willard, refurbished and reopened, is now one of the most expensive hotels in Washington.) He asked me if I would be able to make myself available full time to work on the campaign. I told him that I would like to do that, but could not. I was just concluding an important project for my employer, the Walter E. Heller Company, and the job would not be finished for another several months.

Heller, a large commercial lender, and the Chase Manhattan Bank had made a series of substantial loans to the A. C. Gilbert Company, the toy company famed for Erector Sets and American Flyer trains. The company had defaulted on the loans and the banks decided to liquidate the company. I was designated the lender's representative and was sent to New Haven, Connecticut, for two years, to help supervise the liquidation.

You do not get to be the national president of the Jaycees without being quick on the uptake. I left Skidmore's office having been anointed head of the effort to get Connecticut's 16 delegates to join the Nixon camp. He told me my assignment wouldn't be terribly time consuming. It would consist mostly of keeping each of the delegates informed of Nixon's positions on issues and of current poll results (if positive), and general hand holding.

In 1968, 40 states had primaries or caucuses. At the end of the primary season, it was not clear who was the victor. The candidates went to the national party convention still vying for the nomination. Getting delegates to support your candidate was critical. Every vote counted, even the small group from Connecticut. There were a series of scenarios about how the convention vote might turn out, but a number of them showed Nelson Rockefeller winning and, in theory at least, it was still possible for Ronald Reagan to be the nominee. Nixon was not a sure thing going into the convention.

One of the Connecticut delegates was an attractive lady named Nancy. When I would call her from our apartment in New York City, I would put on my sexiest voice and begin, "HELL-OO, NANCY..." This led Connie to create a line which she still invokes whenever she hears me trying hard to make a point or win someone over to my position. She merely intones in a sultry voice, "HELL-OO, NANCY," and we both get a good chuckle.

After several months of my wooing delegates on the phone, Skidmore invited me to attend the Republican convention in Miami. He told me he would pay for my ticket and hotel room as well as find me a meaningful job. After discussing it with Connie, I took my vacation time from Heller and made plans to attend.

I arrived in Miami and went to the Hilton Hotel to get photographed and to be issued an ID badge. The badge was marked with the number of hotel floors that could be accessed, the top floors being off limits to all but the few senior staff. At the time, these were people whose names were generally unknown to me. I was cleared for the 15th floor only, and not for the next three up, which identified me as being at the bottom of the Nixon totem pole. I only once had occasion to go to the 17th floor, to deliver a short briefing on some aspect of the convention to the Nixon State Chairmen. These important figures were assembled by the Nixon Convention Chairman, a hardnosed lawyer from

Arizona named Richard Kleindienst. (After John Mitchell left the Justice Department, Kleindienst, his deputy, would become the Attorney General of the United States.)

I don't remember the exact subject of the talk that occasioned my visit to the 17th floor, but I remember the room was full of high-powered politicians. I also remember Kleindienst's unintended put-down when he told me, "This is probably the most important day of your life." As I have an abundance of pride, I remember thinking to myself, "how does this SOB know what I have done with my life?" Perhaps he was saving his tact for the donors. My initial impression of Kleindienst was not favorable. Later, when I came to know him, I appreciated his qualities.

The manager of the convention was a gentleman with whom I was unfamiliar, named John Ehrlichman. He ran a very tight operation and I came away impressed by the efficiency of it all.

One incident that occurred during the convention remains fixed in my mind. One of Rally John's team had somehow obtained a pass to the catwalks in the convention center. It was his intention to dress up as an electrician and, when Governor Rockefeller was speaking, get on the catwalk and cut the loudspeaker cables. It didn't sound sportsman-like to me, but Nidecker assured me that it was a common stunt in political campaigning. Nixon, according to Nidecker, had had it done to him in the past, as had Barry Goldwater in 1964. At any rate, the man had coveralls and a belt tool bag and looked the part of an electrician, with one exception. He had a brand new carpenter's claw hammer in his kit. An alert Secret Service agent spotted him as a phony. I never saw or heard of him again in the campaign. Apparently, this was a-one-strike-and-you're-out game.

This incident is indicative of the variety of people and personalities who are attracted to political campaigns and how carefully they need to be monitored and controlled. Nixon would not have condoned such a "dirty trick," but he didn't know about it. Years later, a similarly misguided enthusiast would plan and execute a break-in at the Watergate Hotel.

In Shakespeare's *Julius Caesar*, Brutus tells Cassius:

> There is a tide in the affairs of men, which, taken at the flood, leads on to fortune;
>
> Omitted, all the voyage of their life, is bound in shallows and in miseries.

Nixon won the nomination by 25 votes. I became an advance man on a presidential campaign. I had caught the tide.

2. ADVANCING

With the exception of the fund-raising and delegate efforts, my time in the 1968 presidential campaign was spent as an advance man. I also did some advancing during my White House years, particularly on the larger overseas trips. To fully appreciate some of the stories which follow, one needs to have some understanding of what advancing is all about. I have included this brief description of the duties of an advance man for a front-running presidential candidate. Advancing for the president is much different, and certainly easier, than advancing for a candidate, but it is not without its own set of problems.

While we were in Miami, John Ehrlichman invited me to attend the advance man's school he was running in New York City the following week. Like all other aspects of the Nixon campaign, the school was well organized. It was held at the Waldorf Astoria, lasted a full day, and trained approximately 100 participants. It included a slide show, a televised address from "the candidate" and a manual, a three-ring notebook of over 100 pages with precise instructions on every conceivable aspect of managing campaign stops. This information would be augmented during the weeks before the election with a barrage of telegrams, virtually every day, from the tour office or Ehrlichman. These had the effect, intended or unintended, of magnifying our aura of importance. Every advance man received several telegrams a day, heightening our reputation with the hotel desk personnel.

In essence, the advance man was responsible for everything but security. The campaign tour office scheduled the candidate's visit and respond to policy questions. The Secret Service provided security for the presidential candidates.

The advance man could not commit Nixon to anything that was not on the pre-approved trip plan. The endorsement of the tour office had to be obtained to add or delete events.

The advance man's work started before Nixon's arrival at a city and ended after his departure. We were required to return to the hotel and conduct a "sweep" of the rooms occupied by the senior staff to insure that nothing of consequence had been left behind. (A year later, on the Asian trip, just such a "sweep" found some classified documents in the room that had been occupied by Henry Kissinger.)

The advance man had to accomplish the following:
- arrange with airport authorities for a parking place, away from the terminal, for three Boeing 727s
- build a crowd at the airport
- provide an elevated press platform (four feet high and not facing into the sun)
- arrange for a motorcade with volunteer drivers and cars (gas tanks full); no brand new cars, as they might break down. (The secret service provided a car and driver for the candidate and lead and follow-up security cars.)
- arrange for a baggage truck and baggage handlers
- plan a route from the airport to the hotel or rally (a route designed for political purposes)
- arrange a hotel stop if it was an overnight visit.

No one was to ride in the car with Nixon but his wife or, if one was available, a local democratic leader such as Mayor Daley of Chicago. There were always likely to be more Democrats in an area than Republicans and it made sense to be seen with Democrats. It was not part of the campaign strategy to be seen with other Republicans, no matter how popular they were.

This strategy was not clear to everyone; in Ohio, I once had to literally pull a Congressman from Nixon's car. There is a legend about multi-millionaire J.P. Morgan who supposedly once made an individual rich by walking across the floor of the New York Stock Exchange with his arm across the man's shoulder. Nixon did not wish to share the wealth.

At the hotel, the specific instructions in the advance man's notebook included a number of sections on room placement for the 300 staff and press. We were kept jumping, to organize and monitor such details as:
- who was on what floor (pre-registered, keys in envelopes with names on them)
- staff offices (ten typewriters) with food service
- background curtains in press briefing room (blue, folded, not pleated)

- press rooms with typewriters (10, manual) food and beverages (alcoholic and non-), telephones (25).

There were notebook sections on crowd (rally) building, advertising, setting up telephone boiler shops to get out the party faithful, public address equipment, and lighting for TV cameras (3200 Kelvin), etc. If an elephant was to be used at a rally, he had to have an enema before the event. This admonition discouraged me from ever planning the use of even a small pachyderm.

The size of the rally was very important. Bodies were all that mattered. We knew the press didn't count only those old enough to vote. In Boise, Idaho, I got the schools closed so that every child could attend Nixon's speech. On another advance, the tour office had scheduled Cleveland on a Saturday morning. I selected the most popular shopping mall for the rally site and ended up with 15,000 people. Many of them, I suspect, were just curious K Mart shoppers. The effect was spectacular.

You had to be an impresario. We used bands, popular entertainers, balloons, signs and movie stars to build excitement. The rally was not important for its own sake but for the 15 seconds of television time it might earn if it were successful and the footage was picked up by the TV networks. The days of speaking to crowds in order to try to reach the American public were long gone. It was TV time, TV time and TV time that mattered. Everything else was a means to that end.

The manual covered how to set up the podium and who could be on it. Nixon wanted to be *the* star political personage. He did not wish to share the platform with people running for every local office, from dog-catcher to mayor, trying to tap into our crowd-building success. It was our stage and we were taught to share it with as few people as possible.

Ehrlichman had explicit directions on what the candidate would do: shake hands with the hotel manager, and pose for a picture with the motorcycle outriders *if* the advance man lined them up at the airplane. What he would not do: kiss babies, pose for pictures, or give impromptu speeches. Most importantly, he would not wear a hat, cap, helmet or Indian headdress. Nixon claimed, "only guys running for sheriff wear funny hats." (Years later, Governor Dukakis, running for president, posed in an armored vehicle and a tanker's helmet. The visual effect confirmed Nixon's sense that it could do no good. The press ridiculed him and it was a distinct turning point for his campaign.)

All of the activities from start to finish had to be timed precisely. John Ehrlichman, as the tour director, did not accept planning in greater than five-minute blocks. It was the advance man's job to establish a schedule and hold the candidate to it. When Nixon arrived at a stop, the advance man was in charge. It was his city. He told Ehrlichman when Nixon should stop "working the fence," shaking hands, etc., and move on to the next stop.

By running the campaign on time, our organization was often contrasted by the press to the more casual scheduling of the Democratic candidate Hubert Humphrey. We liked to say, "the ability to run a good campaign doesn't predict anything about an administration, but the inability to do so has to tell you something." In Boston, while working on a Nixon advance, I attended a Humphrey rally and introduced myself to the advance man in charge. He invited me to sit with him and listen to Humphrey's speech. I got to feeling sorry for the poor fellow when Hubert ran well over his allotted time. It was the advance man's responsibility to see that the schedule was kept; but the candidate has to cooperate. Nixon was very aware of this and respected the judgment of his advance men.

I remember an episode in one of the C.S. Forester books which describes Horatio Hornblower in his first command. He visits a small, impoverished South American country which had just allied itself with the British Government. Hornblower sails into the harbor, meets with the local ruler and presents his replenishment requirements: 30 quintals of salt, 10 casks of rum, 20 bullocks, 100 casks of salt pork, and so on. The poor man is simply overwhelmed. He has just become a friend of the King of England and the first test of that friendship will bankrupt his treasury. It is a poignant description and one that went through my mind every time I went to a new city and met with the local Republican leaders: "20 cars with drivers, 20 volunteers to assist at the hotel, 10 baggage handlers with trucks, copies of the local newspaper the day we arrive in every room plus 50 for the press room, a PA system for the rally and another for the press room, podiums decorated with red, white and blue bunting, 3,000 helium balloons, 500 hand-lettered signs, 2 bands, a phone bank operation with 50 phones and volunteers to man them; and the list went on. A successful overnight stop, with a rally, required legions of volunteer assistants to pull it off. This could put a strain on even the largest Republican organization.

Further, as we were instructed to have the local Republican committee absorb as much of the cost as possible, the advance man had the potential to become *persona non grata* very quickly. There were stories among the advance staff of cities to which they could never return. The County Chairman had a "contract" out on them for spending money and having the bills sent to the local party.

In the fall of 1968, Nixon was crisscrossing the country and sometimes making several stops a day so there were a number of advance men involved. Usually, if it were a city with an overnight stay (RON, "remain overnight," in advance man's parlance), you were given a week to ten days to arrange things. Smaller stops, such as my afternoon rally in Boise, Idaho, may involve a week or less. No matter how simple the stop, if a rally was involved, time was required to execute the advertising, set up the phone bank and otherwise coordinate logistics.

To be a successful, an advance man had to possess certain characteristics. Advancing was an 18-hour-a-day job, seven days a week; physical, mental and emotional stamina were critical. You had to be quick-thinking, decisive and enjoy being in command. You had to be creative. Most importantly, you had be the kind of person whose motto in life was, "first we get into the stadium, then we change for better seats." Charles Dickens's *artful dodger* would have been perfect.

When I joined the campaign, I was commuting from New York City to New Haven, Connecticut, where I was involved in liquidating the A.C. Gilbert Co. I remember describing the functions of an advance man to an older fellow, one of the retired managers, who listened carefully and then said: "You know, that sounds just like the advance men the circuses used to have when I was a boy." Upon reflection, I agreed.

It *was* just like the circus.

3. OUT OF THE BOX

There is an old expression that states: "Once you get a reputation as an early riser, you can sleep as late as you wish." As I have remained an early riser throughout my entire working career, I cannot speak to the validity of this theory. I can, however, attest with authority to the value of establishing a reputation early on.

My first advance trip was to Houston, Texas. It would turn out to be a serendipitous place to start my education. The tour office in New York City had specified an arrival rally at the airport, a small arrival rally at the hotel and a big, nighttime, outdoor rally in downtown Houston. There was also a "fat cat" gathering in the evening before the outdoor event. Edward L. Morgan was assigned as the experienced teacher. John Brown, a young man on loan from the Koppers Company in Pittsburgh and I were the acolytes. Instead of each of us being involved in everything, we parceled out the responsibilities. John got the airport, I got the rally and Morgan took the hotel.

The advance man's manual called for us to work with the local Republican Party officials and have them designate counterparts to be our assistants. Accordingly, Robert Mosbacher, a wealthy oil wildcatter who was later to become President Bush's (the first) Secretary of Commerce, was picked to be the overall visit chairman. Mosbacher would also keep the Washington gossip columnists happy with the never-ending copy provided by his flamboyant second wife, Georgette. For my counterpart, I drew one of the heirs to the Standard Oil fortune, a close friend and hunting partner of President Bush (the first), Will

Farrish. Will drove an Aston Martin and carried the first pager I had ever seen. Come to think of it, it may also have been the first real Aston Martin I had seen.

We selected as a site for the outdoor rally a large open-air auditorium in a park in downtown Houston. This was one of those affairs where the overhead shell covers the stage and an acre or so of seating, but has an overflow capacity on out to about the range of an average lady's golf drive. It was immense. I told Farrish that we were going to have put on quite a show to attract a crowd large enough to fill the place. He told me not to worry about money: get whomever and whatever I needed to do it right.

I had a list of telephone numbers of Republican movie stars and show business personalities. Then, as now, it was not a very long list; but John Wayne topped it. I can still remember my excitement when I dialed the private number and found myself talking to the "Duke." Wayne couldn't make the event, but I collared some lesser luminaries. Farrish arranged for a private plane to fetch them from Hollywood or Las Vegas or wherever they were located. As a former advertising man from New York, I put together a media buy that would have made Procter and Gamble jealous, but Farrish didn't blink. I think if I had requested the New York Philharmonic or a jump by the 101st Airborne Division, I would have been accommodated.

The rally was a smash success, with great throngs of people. Nixon was so animated by the crowd that he stopped the motorcade as it was leaving. He got out of his car and climbed on the hood, waving his arms, his forefingers and middle fingers spread in the familiar Churchill/Eisenhower/Nixon "V for Victory" sign, surrounded by cheering, ecstatic supporters. It was electrifying.

Nixon sent for me the next morning. It was the first time I had actually met him. He told me that my first rally "out of the box" was the largest night-time political event he had ever seen, and thanked me for my efforts. My reputation was established. I was golden.

Napoleon once observed that he wanted "Generals who were lucky." I didn't fully appreciate it at the time, but my drawing Houston, Mosbacher and Farrish for my first advance was pure luck. It is amazing what one can do with an unlimited budget and a "can do" attitude on the part of the local organization, not to mention some powerful players.

We stayed overnight at the Shamrock Hilton, an old flagship of the Hilton chain. It was constructed on a large piece of ground on the edge of Houston with a long curving driveway, ideal for forming motorcades. Apparently, the Shamrock bar was the headquarters for all the wildcatters and oil men in

Houston in the 50s and 60s. It also had an enormous swimming pool with a 10-meter diving platform. After the candidate's plane left (or, later, the president's) it was customary for the political advance man and the advance Secret Service agent to hold a "wheels up" party, to recognize and pay homage to the patron saint of advance men for a successful visit with no untoward events. The agent and I had evoked this practice and were sitting beside the pool at the Hilton, probably drinking more than was good for us. In one of those moments of youthful braggadocio, he challenged me to go off the 10-meter board. I said I would, if he would. Together we climbed up to the top, at the same level as the third story of the hotel, and looked down. The water was shimmering, crystal clear. The bottom of the pool was some 15 feet below the surface, so the visual effect was of a 45 foot height. Other revelers around the pool were watching us and, embarrassing as it was, it was probably the only proof that our brains were still working when we decided to slink carefully back down.

I read in *Newsweek* that the Shamrock Houston, landmark that it was, was torn down in the 1980s to make way for a new housing development. It was a grand hotel, but whenever I think of it I can only remember the pool and the 10-meter board.

I will also remember the young Houston congressman I met. He was running for the Senate and when I got home to New York, I told my wife all about him. He had his own oil company, and was different from most other members of Congress. He was not at all pretentious; just a nice guy. I told Connie that this was a man with a future.

The Congressman lost his run for the Senate but I followed his career with more than a little interest, as I was sure he would go far. Nixon first made him the head of the Republican Party, then the Ambassador to the United Nations, followed by the head of the Liaison Office to the Peoples Republic of China. President Ford made him the head of the CIA. Later, he served with distinction in the administration of Ronald Reagan. Finally in 1988, he struck out on his own.

In 1968, George Herbert Walker Bush definitely had a future.

4. TWO CAR FUNERALS

After our major success in Houston, Ed Morgan and I were assigned to do an overnight stop in Cleveland, Ohio. We were working together again, with a schedule that specified an arrival rally at the airport and a big Saturday morning rally. Then it was back to the hotel until the evening, when Nixon had a *Man in the Arena* TV show scheduled. Again, we divided the responsibilities. Ed took the arrival, the hotel and the TV show. With my previous success in crowd building fresh on our minds, I got the rally.

Generating crowds is not an easy business, particularly on a Saturday morning when people are sleeping in, having big breakfasts or doing chores around the house. Generally, people have to be collected and placed in position in a sort of "crowd seeding" operation. If you can get a small crowd to form, and there are enough other people in the area, you will always attract a larger number of people through curiosity alone. That is the first law of crowd building.

A sidebar about crowds and reporters:

Unlike "the flowers that bloom in the spring," crowds and demonstrations are not natural occurrences. Whether it is a political rally for Richard Nixon, a riot protesting the World Bank or a demonstration against the US war in Iraq, they don't just happen. They are all carefully planned. You just don't turn out thousands of people carrying signs, singing chants and marching down a fixed route. Somewhere, lurking in the background, is an advance man, or a team of advance men. No large crowds are spontaneous. They are *all* organized. They are created by the sponsoring organization for the benefit of television and news people, who seem to fall for the "behind the scenes" effort every time.

I have considerable respect for American journalists when it comes to investigative reporting. I have no respect for them when it comes to their understanding how they are being manipulated by the crowd builders. There is no excitement in filming thousands of people at home; the cameras and the reporters naturally focus upon the mass of people in front of them. News people probably understand domestic political campaigns pretty well, and the role of the advance staff. Sometimes they are even cynical about them. They just don't seem to extrapolate this experience into other types of crowd situations. As a former advance man, I find that surprising. Reporters should give more credit to the organizers of the event and not fall victim to the carefully manufactured image they present.

There is *one* place that families tend to flock to of their own volition on Saturdays; the shopping mall. I chose the biggest mall in the area and sought out the manager. I told him I would like to put up a stage in his parking lot for a visit, the following Saturday, of the next president of the United States. He bought into the idea as though it were his own.

The star of a TV western show (it was the late 60s and cowboy shows were popular) was named Drury. The name of the show I have long forgotten, but Drury was a Nixon fan. I arranged for him to arrive by stagecoach. Along with a country band, he would entertain the crowd before Nixon arrived. No, I do not recall where I found a stagecoach in Cleveland, Ohio, either.

But I can still remember the stagecoach coming through the parking lot, surrounded by an estimated 15,000 people, with our cowboy on top, waving his ten gallon hat. Cecil B. De Mille would have been proud. Nixon was energized. It was the last good thing I would do that day.

The English language is rich with slang expressions denoting incompetence and ineptitude; "could screw up a crowbar in a sandbox" and "couldn't pour pee out of a boot if the instructions were printed on the heel," are two such examples. They add color to our speech and usually describe an act of such an exaggerated nature as to be inapplicable to even the worst dumb-dumb.

Anyone who has ever been an advance man will tell you that the organization and operation of motorcades is one of the most difficult of the campaign functions; the more cars, the more difficult the problem. In the 1968 campaign, our typical lineup for a motorcade was as follows:

1. Motorcycle outriders, supplied by local police
2. Lead police car or cars
3. Advance security car driven by Secret Service
4. Candidate's car
5. Follow up security car driven by Secret Service
6. Wire Service (AP & UP) car
7. Photographers' car
8. H & H car (Haldeman & Higby)
9. Ehrlichman car
10. Staff cars (as many as six)
11. Press buses (usually three, although by the end of the campaign there were as many as six)

At airport arrivals, these vehicles would be lined up on the tarmac and we always pulled it off without a hitch. The cars were all marked and everyone knew where they belonged. However, as Nixon usually stayed overnight in top hotels, located in the heart of a city, with minimum parking and crowded streets, problems could, and did, occur with downtown motorcades. Obtaining cars and drivers and coordinating them in those pre-cell phone days was always a challenge.

In Cleveland, candidate Nixon had built "staff time" into his schedule the afternoon after the rally. My only responsibility was to deliver Mrs. Nixon to a local TV station for an interview. Several days before the arrival, I ran the route from the hotel to the station with my Secret Service counterpart. We agreed that a two-car motorcade would be sufficient. Cleveland would supply a police car in which the agent and I would ride. Behind us would be Mrs. Nixon's car, driven by a secret service agent, with her personal agent as a passenger in the front seat. Cleveland also supplied two motorcycle police outriders to lead the motorcade. The route was a little tricky as it involved going past the station and coming around the block in order to accommodate a one-way street and end up at the entrance to the TV station.

The departure from the hotel was flawless, but when we got to the road that we were supposed to pass, the motorcycle outriders turned. The result of this failure was that we ended up across a busy urban street from the entrance to the TV station. At this point, their error sunk in and the hapless riders had to block traffic so we could execute a U turn, with backing and filling, in the middle of the block, and discharge Mrs. Nixon on a sidewalk. I was mortified.

There is another old description of ineptitude with which I have long been familiar. "He could screw up a two-car funeral."

If a two-car motorcade is anything like a two-car funeral, I qualify.

5. THE HERO OF BOISE

After Cleveland, Ed and I split up. He went to Seattle to do an overnight. I was assigned Boise, Idaho with an afternoon rally. Nixon had two earlier stops in the day, Sioux Falls S.D. and Bismarck, N.D. He would do Boise and then go on to Seattle, Washington.

This was my first test alone and I was eager to do everything perfectly. Fortunately, Boise is a long way from anything and therefore the local folks are eager for excitement. Also, it was Nixon country. My local chairman was a man named Bill Campbell, the Will Farrish equivalent in Boise. I was again virtually guaranteed of success. Having Nixon visit was the biggest thing that had happened in Boise since the first Potato Queen Contest.

I got the steps to the state capitol set up for a speech and filled the park in front of it with people, including all of the school kids in the county. Instead of bringing Nixon straight through the crowd, I roped off a zig-zag route through the trees and brought Nixon through an eight-foot aisle behind which were people and kids, standing six deep, on both sides. It was the largest crowd anyone had ever seen in Boise. My reputation as a rally man was growing. Some days later, when I got into an elevator with Nixon, Ehrlichman and Haldeman, Bob called me "the hero of Boise."

As the Seattle stop was after Boise, I hitched a ride on the campaign plane to be of whatever help I could to Ed Morgan. I had flown up the weekend before to give him a hand for several days, after I was confident of success in Boise. I was hoping that we would both be assigned to another big city. I enjoyed his company and we got along well together.

In Seattle, Nixon had to walk down a long pier get on a Lockheed Corporation hovercraft and take a test ride. The officials at Lockheed were all in hard hats and wanted Nixon to wear, one too, but Morgan said no. He knew full well that he would be held responsible, and would catch hell from Ehrlichman. Or Haldeman. Or Nixon. Or all three. The Lockheed people insisted and Nixon put one on when he arrived. He took it off, minutes later, knowing that none of the Lockheed management would dare to make him replace it.

As the mass of the press corps was walking down the pier, I noticed a woman reporter who was wearing a large badge with an outline of a bird in a sort of a block silhouette form. I didn't recognize it and asked her what the badge was.

She proceeded to inform me, in excruciating detail, about Cesar Chavez, the leader of the migrant workers' movement in California. The pin was his emblem, the Thunderbird. She was clearly not an unbiased observer. I stoically stood for this harangue for a few minutes and then made a smart-ass remark; she took great offence. Later, in her article, *"Learning to Live with Nixon"* for the *New York* magazine, Gloria Steinem would refer to me as a typical BMOC (big man on campus). As that was a level I had never achieved in college, I took it as a compliment.

6. NEVER TRUST A LOCAL

Nixon spent October 3, 1968 in Atlanta. The tour office had scheduled a parade in the heart of the city on Peachtree Street and ending in front of the Hyatt Regency Hotel, the first of architect John Portman's 20-story atrium designs. As it was one of two parades planned in a major city for the 1968 campaign, the campaign headquarters back in New York wanted a "barn burner." Because of the parade, and because big city stops were complicated, and because we had asked to work together whenever possible, the tour office had assigned Ed Morgan and myself to do the Atlanta advance: two heavyweights, as we now liked to think of ourselves. Somewhere between Houston, Seattle and Cleveland, Ed and I had become best friends. We were kindred spirits.

The airport arrival was typical and it went without problems: arrange with airport authorities for parking for three Boeing 727 aircraft, build a press platform out of flat bed trailers; separate an area with a fence. Stock it with a half dozen bus loads of party faithful. Set up a motorcade adjacent to the end of the fence. I could do it in my sleep.

The hotel stop was a pleasure. The staff at the Hyatt Hotel were professional, experienced and accommodating. They understood the need for press rooms with an endless supply of food, tele-printers, extra phones, quick cleaning service, staff lounges, staff offices and all of the other requests we laid on them. It all came together. Even the parade was easier to organize than we predicted.

The city officials were most gracious and allowed us to hang signs from the light poles along the parade route. I bought 1000 yards of four-foot wide unbleached muslin and got a Young Republican organization to paint a continuous message. On the night before the parade, the banner was hung with the aid of a rented cherry-picker truck. We distributed notices to all of the office buildings along the route. We were able to specify the time that Nixon would be at their location with confidence, because John Ehrlichman, the tour director, demanded *exact* adherence to the agreed upon schedule.

The parade went well, with huge throngs of people, and we were pleased. At the end of the parade, the cars were all parked in the basement garage of the Hyatt. It was impossible to segregate a block of space, but the drivers tried to get the cars close together and in some kind of order. Then the drivers were sent to a special lounge we had established for them and they were warned not to wander off. They had a groaning board full of fancy sandwiches and soft drinks, and several TVs. Their creature comforts had been attended to. They were to stay put for some five hours when their services would again be needed, as Nixon had to go to a TV station for a *Man in the Arena* production. This was a TV show in which Nixon answered questions from a panel, in front of an audience. The station was on the outskirts of Atlanta, some 30 minutes away.

Approximately 45 minutes before the scheduled departure, Ed Morgan and I went to the drivers' lounge to start organizing the motorcade. We had obtained the cooperation of the Atlanta police and had permission to double-park on Peachtree Street. The drivers knew to which cars they were assigned and where they belonged in the motorcade. Or, so we thought.

There are numerous popular axioms and aphorisms that address events that evolve in a manner other than anticipated, Murphy's Law perhaps being the most well known; "If something can go wrong, it will." I am particularly fond of O'Reilly's corollary, "Murphy was an optimist." The advance men in 1968 had refined Murphy, O'Reilly and other such philosophy into a single phrase: "never trust a local." By "local" we meant anyone who was not a part of the Nixon campaign staff. It was a guiding principle and its utility would be proven again and again.

When we got to the lounge, it was deserted. Our volunteers had partaken of our hospitality and split. The sandwiches were gone and so were the drivers.

Panic. If I had to come up with one word which described my emotions at that time, panic is it. Richard Nixon expected to leave the hotel in 45 minutes and we had no motorcade drivers. There was nothing to do but get new ones. Of course, we could have gotten members of the staff to drive, but that would have left us with the motorcade cars at the airport, as Nixon was flying out after the TV show. It also would have exposed our failure.

Somewhere in Atlanta a dozen citizens probably are still talking about the evening in 1968 when they were accosted on the street by a tall guy in a suit who asked if they were willing to drive in a Nixon campaign motorcade. Morgan was in the garage sending up cars with the attendants while I was lining up the cars on the street and staffing them with new volunteer drivers. It was a race against time. As the appointed hour for departure approached, we were almost ready. John Ehrlichman was on the radio every couple of minutes demanding to know what was happening. I was stalling him by saying that I was having some difficulties with lining up my motorcade. As a former advance man himself, he would understand that. He would *never* understand the total loss of drivers.

Finally, the job was accomplished. The motorcade was in order, the drivers told to follow the car ahead of them. The reporters were in their buses. The clutch of staff had arrived and loaded. Under normal circumstances the advance man was responsible to fetch the candidate and escort him to his car. We didn't have time for that. I radioed John Ehrlichman and told him to bring Nixon down. Morgan and I jumped in the lead police car. The motorcycles roared, the sirens wailed and the roof lights flashed. We were off.

Neither Ed Morgan nor I ever divulged how close to disaster we came that day. Now, all of the principals who were involved, Nixon, Haldeman, Ehrlichman, and Morgan are gone. This is, to my knowledge, the first public admission of the incident.

Where did the drivers disappear? We never found out, but Ed and I both believed that our volunteer drivers were really Humphrey people who had infiltrated the local Nixon campaign organization. Dirty tricks didn't start with Watergate. The so-called "black advance" was perfected by the Democratic Party's lead advance man, the famous Dick Tuck. His tricks and antics were the stuff of legends. Tuck was a real hero to Bob Haldeman, who was forever hoping one of his troops would be as creative. Tuck once dressed in a railroad brakeman's suit and signaled the engineer to pull out of the station while some poor Republican office seeker was speaking from the rear deck of the observation car. And, the poor Republican was Richard Nixon.

In political advancing, as in life, it is not so much *keeping* out of trouble that is important. It is knowing how *to get out of it* that counts. Ed and I had proved ourselves equal to the task. We had also tested the validity of the advance man's dictum, "Never trust a local," and not found it wanting.

7. Betrayal in Boston

Ken Cole, the campaign tour manager in New York City, was apologetic. He was short of advance men. I would have to do Boston alone. It was late in October and some of the advance men in the original group had not panned out; others had to return to their primary employment. He had nobody to help me. He knew that a major city with an overnight stop normally called for a two-man team, as the airport arrival, hotel and event were just too much for one man, but as he said I would just have to do the best I could. "Oh, and one other thing. We don't have a hotel locked in."

I flew into Boston a week before the visit and checked into the Hilton, the preferred hotel whenever one was available. When I got to my room, I called the manager, identified myself and asked if I could come down and meet with him. In a few minutes I was sitting in front of the manager's desk and stating my case. I wanted a special price for 300 rooms for one night. What could he do for me? Hotels usually break even at around 65% of capacity and average about 80%; thus, filling them to 100% usually warranted a significant discount. There were also the extra rents obtained from the press rooms, lounges, offices and the prestige of having a presidential candidate. Hotels were usually eager for our business.

"Mr. Stuart," he intoned, "I can't do anything for you. I am booked up all next week with a very large convention." "Not a problem," was my first reaction. Boston is a big city with lots of hotels. "We'll go to the Marriott." The manager continued to speak. "And I am afraid that all of the other major hotels are sold out, too. You are going to have trouble finding 50 rooms, much less 300." The full import of Cole's remark, "we don't have a hotel locked in," began to become clear.

I went back to my room and called the tour office. What did they want me to do? Their response was the same as Cole's first comment: "do your best." The trip to Boston had already been announced and it was the only trip planned for Massachusetts. They couldn't remove it from the schedule.

Most big cities, particularly older ones, have a number of small, aging, second-class hotels. After spending the afternoon on the phone, I managed to put together a half dozen of them, including one that would work as the headquarters and had a decent suite for Nixon. It currently had a tour group occupying most of its 185 rooms, but they were checking out at noon on the same day that the campaign would be arriving at 3:00. I would have to put together a shuttle service between the other hotels and the headquarters. The press would be unhappy, but there was little choice. With great relief, I started on the rest of my tasks.

I called the State Republican Chairman and scheduled a meeting for the next day. I told him to bring a lot of volunteers. With six hotels, we would need them.

Massachusetts is, of course, Kennedy country and the Republican Party was very small. Small, I was to find out, but rabid. When I told them this was to be the only visit to their state, they became aggravated and wanted to know why. When, after much backing and filling on my part, I told them the truth — that we had already written off Massachusetts — they became enraged. Then, when I told them that we couldn't risk an outdoor rally because of Boston's huge population of liberal college students who would demonstrate against the Vietnam War at the drop of an English 101 text, they went mad. They wanted to know who was making these misguided decisions, and they wanted to know who was my boss. The fact is, the tour office had only scheduled a *Man in the Arena* presentation and I agreed with them wholeheartedly. An outdoor rally in Boston would be political suicide. In deference to the Massachusetts campaign workers, I did relent and talked to the tour office, which agreed to allow me to rent an indoor hall so that the workers could at least see Nixon. (Nixon lost Massachusetts in 1968 *and* in 1972, when it was the only state which, along with the District of Columbia, was carried by McGovern.)

I guess, to be a Republican in Massachusetts, you had to be a little extreme, but I finally got the group settled down and assigned them their responsibilities. For the local chairman I tapped a man named Clifford DeMotte, who turned out to be extraordinarily helpful. I was very happy to recommend him later for a job in Washington with one of the government agencies.

By dint of great effort, Cliff and I were able to arrange the airport arrival and motorcade, set up the HQ hotel and the shuttle service. We would have some complications with the press corps, as they normally stayed in one hotel. We assigned rooms and made up a roster, with a copy for everyone of the traveling staff and press.

My wife was producing a film on location in Cape Cod and I inveigled her to come down and set up a press meeting for Mrs. Nixon and the local "newsies." I also asked her to pick up Billy Graham's daughter at the airport, as she was flying in to be with Tricia and Julie. The Nixon daughters didn't travel full time with their parents, but were joining their mother and father in Boston. I still had a lot to do, but on the day before the arrival I was confident that things were under control.

Then, at about 4:00 PM, on the day before the landing of the three 727s, the hotel manager at the HQ hotel informed me, without a bit of shame or embarrassment (he must have been one of the Democrats) that his tour group was staying over another day and that he could only give me approximately 50 rooms. I had less than 24 hours to line up 135 rooms in a city in which I had already snatched up every room in every hotel that wasn't a hot bed operation. I called up Cole and asked him to immediately detach a traveling press aide named Tim Elbourne from wherever he was. I needed help.

Tim was a very likeable fellow, on loan from the Walt Disney organization. His job on the tour, along with another individual named Bruce Whelihan, was the care and feeding of the two plane-loads of traveling press corps. Elbourne and Whelihan moved with the press, answered their questions, got them on buses on time, located lost baggage and generally tried to keep them happy. It was a big job and an important one. Reporters are human. Missing a bus could result in anger and emotional deterioration that could ultimately manifest itself in a critical story. Keeping the press engaged and satisfied was critical.

Elbourne arrived later that evening and we spent the night calling hotels out on Cape Cod, as far as 40 miles away, arranging for a bus service and redoing the room rosters. We had the press corps spread out over "hell's half acre," but it couldn't be helped.

The Nixon portion of the visit went fine. The student population of Boston, hindered by our choice of hotels, never found out where we were. As a result, there were no demonstrations. Connie's efforts on behalf of Mrs. Nixon turned out well and would be remembered, later. As for me, it didn't matter what hotel I was in as there was no chance of getting a moment's rest.

8. MORGAN AND MADISON SQUARE

After the debacle in the second battle of Cleveland (see Chapter 33) I was invited to ride back to New York on the *Tricia*, the name painted on the nose of the Nixon's 727 airplane. This was partly as a sop to make me feel good and partly because Bob Haldeman wanted to talk to me. Also, Ed Morgan had asked for my return to New York as soon as possible to help with the big, final rally scheduled for the old Madison Square Garden. Not the old, old, old Madison Square Garden, built in 1874 on Madison Square, or the old, old Garden, built in 1890, but the old Madison Square Garden of 1925, at 7th Avenue and 30th Street. There is now a new Madison Square Garden at the same location. But it is not the same. It has been modernized, sanitized and glamorized to the point where a 50s Friday night fight fan wouldn't feel welcome. The Garden has such a rich history in New York that I am sure there will always be one somewhere in the city.

The tour office wanted to end the campaign with a dramatically successful indoor rally in New York, the home base of our campaign operation and the TV networks, who were sure to give the event good coverage. The problem was that New York City was not Nixon Country. It was hippy country. The York City police department was afraid there was going to be a major anti-war protest. So were we. Ed was given the job of creating a demonstration-free environment for the last hurrah of the 1968 campaign. He succeeded beyond anyone's expectations.

Morgan was, according to John Ehrlichman, the most creative of the advance men. He was also certainly the wittiest and probably the brightest. Ed was a constant hoot, a funny observation a minute. These were delivered in droll voice, with little or no change in facial expression except a twinkle in the eye and sometimes a slight upturn of the mouth, the beginnings of a grin. And, because he was very, very smart, there was an intellectual element that is usually absent in most humorists. He had a British sense of humor without being a Brit. These characteristics were appreciated by John Ehrlichman, but did not endear him to Bob Haldeman, who really didn't like wisecracking advance men.

Ed was slightly out of proportion, a long legged, big man, some 6' 4" tall who carried himself in a sort of stooped over, round-shouldered posture that emphasized his extra weight. He was, however, very fast on his feet, as I found out in a game of one-on-one basketball after the campaign. His coordination was excellent. He had the long fingered, fine hands of a magician, which he was, and he enjoyed doing card tricks and sleights. When he extracted a cigarette from the pack in his shirt pocket, it was in one fluid motion. He would reach in behind his jacket, extend one thin finger into the pack, and drag out a cigarette as though his finger were a magnet and the butt was a scrap of iron. I must have seen him do this several hundred times and it impressed me every time.

Ed was always "on," but only infrequently "up," as he was, I believe, somewhat naturally depressed. He had split with his wife over her unhappiness with his Republican advancing aspirations. Later, she was unwilling to come to Washington with him. She had no desire to participate in the political life that was so exciting to Ed. She wished to go on in a comfortable life in Phoenix where Ed was the litigating partner in the best law firm. He was, I learned from others, somewhat of a legal superstar. He had been asked to run for the Office of Arizona Attorney General by the State Republican Party, before he was 30. He had chosen not to do so, but he was held in high esteem in legal circles and would undoubtedly have an extremely promising career. As a lightning-fast thinker, he delighted in mind games. We once played *B for Botticelli* for two hours straight. This mental quickness, honed in jury trials, was the skill he brought to advancing.

The Garden management provided tickets for the existing number of seats, I think about 14,000. To insure that this protocol would be observed, their official tickets had some colored threads running through the cardboard. When the ticket takers tore the tickets, they could determine if they were real or counterfeit. Ed expected advance men to be the ticket takers, so he promptly had 20,000 extra tickets printed. The plan was to distribute the official tickets to the Republican organizations in the suburbs and New Jersey. The other tickets would be spread around the city to insure a full house. This was done without the knowledge of the New York City Fire Marshall or the Garden management. The only problem was that there was a high probability, indeed, a certainty, that some of these tickets would find their way into the hands of protestors intent on disrupting the Nixon festivities. Here, Ed's genius was demonstrated.

Ed rented a large empty office several blocks away and decorated it with Nixon campaign posters. He also had some special signs made which proclaimed the office to be the "Nixon Ticket Headquarters." When the advance men/ticket takers took, and tore, a ticket from someone who didn't look like a Nixon Republican, they were told that their ticket was counterfeit and they couldn't be admitted. They were then told they could go to the nearby ticket office and would be given real tickets. When they arrived at the office, they were informed that all the tickets on hand had been distributed, but more were on the way over and "would be there shortly." Needless to say, more tickets never arrived.

To control the flow of entrants to the ticket takers, Ed had long wooden chutes constructed, one person wide, so that the advance men executing the winnowing process were protected. They could perform their selection task without being surrounded by angry people who had been rejected. When a young man with a beard, long hair, grubby or otherwise of disreputable appearance or a girl with obvious hippy propensities got to the ticket takers, they were refused admittance. If they objected, and many did, there were other advance men standing by to help ease them along in the process. Ed wanted me, along with some of the other big men, to be one of the enforcers. Occasionally, there was a real argument and some tugging, pulling and pushing, but fortunately there were about a dozen advance men and the suspects weren't in the line *en masse*.

I went with Ed to One Police Plaza, the Headquarters of the NYPD, to a final coordination meeting with the senior police officials. At the time, New York had some 28,000 officers, the approximate equivalent of two army divisions. On the night of the rally, it seemed they were all in the neighborhood of the Garden. They helped us by weeding out groups of militants and obvious demonstrators carrying signs. They didn't want a riot on their hands, either.

There was only one fish that got through the net. Shortly after Nixon started his speech, a demonstrator on an upper level unrolled a banner that he had wrapped around his body, and hung it over the edge of the balcony. However, Morgan had foreseen that possibility and had stationed flying squads of men with radios around the Garden. The banner-man got the bum's rush as 20 guys in suits descended upon him.

I personally saw no harm in our little ruse. Nixon wanted to speak without disruption. It was a private party and the protestors were not invited. I did see one incident that disturbed me, however.

Several advance men from the Midwest were shoving four young Jewish men around, pulling them out of a chute. There were great protestations, as only New Yorkers can do. These fellows wore beards and yarmulkes which clearly were not recognized as signs of membership in a religious group. They were, to the advance men, just a bunch of freaks in beards and beanies. I was thankful there were no photographers around, that time.

By the time the ticket seekers gave up the wait at the phony office and returned to the Garden, the seating capacity had been reached. The fire marshals had stopped admitting anyone, real or counterfeit.

9. THE ELECTION

During the final weeks before the election, Nixon's ratings in the polls began to slip. In the third week of October, he had led Hubert Humphrey in the Gallup poll by eight points. But, by the end of that month, when Lyndon Johnson announced the bombing halt in Vietnam, the lead had slipped to two points, 42 to 40, in the same poll. Finally, on the day before the election, the Harris organization showed Humphrey leading Nixon 43 to 40.

Election day dawned bright and clear in New York. After I voted, I hung around our apartment, following the returns on television with the same degree of interest that one accords the warm-ups before the NCAA final in basketball. They are interesting to watch, but hardly an insight into the outcome.

When evening approached, it was nail-biting time. Nixon and Humphrey were in a dead heat. As Connie and I dressed for the "victory" party at the Waldorf Astoria, I was in a state of high unrest.

First of all, I was fatigued. I had endured several months of operating under a great deal of pressure, with only limited sleep. I had been on a continual emotional high, running on adrenalin. Now, the organ manufacturing that chemical had abruptly shut down.

Secondly, I was perplexed. I had a good career going for myself at Heller. The day before the election, I had even shown up at the office and told my boss that I would be back for duty the following week. I had taken my leave of absence with every intention of returning. When I left Heller, I had no desire to go to work for the government. In fact, I had a low opinion of the government bureaucracy. I could not imagine working in Washington. I always envisioned myself as an entrepreneur and was at Heller to learn about corporate finance. Still, I had just finished a job that offered tremendous excitement. I knew that working at Heller would be somewhat hum-drum after the buzz of the campaign. Finally, Bob Haldeman's words to me on the plane coming back from Cleveland: "Tell me about yourself. We're going to need people like you on the White House staff," continued to play games with my mind. What if...?

The party at the Waldorf for the advance men and traveling campaign staff was in recognition of a job well done. There was a large private room with drinks, food and a band. All of the guys from around the country were there, with their wives. By this time I knew many of them, and many more by their reputations (good and bad). We considered ourselves the Delta Force of the Nixon campaign, the men who made things happen, the championship team in a game that had been played over several months.

We introduced our wives, ate, drank, carried on and watched the returns coming in. At 1:30 AM, with no clear victory in sight, Connie and I decided to go back home and wait until the morrow to find out who our new president would be. I went to bed not knowing who won but, hoping against hope, I had a deep down feeling of confidence that Nixon would prevail.

The next morning Connie called me to the television at around 7:00 to watch Herb Klein, Nixon's Director of Communications, on the TV networks, announcing that Nixon had won. Humphrey conceded at 11:30 in the morning. We dressed and returned to the grand ballroom of the Waldorf Astoria for Nixon's appearance at 12:30 PM.

Richard Nixon had received 43.4% of the vote, Humphrey 42.72%, a difference of slightly less than 500,000 out of 73,000,000 votes cast. Not the closest election in history, but too close for everyone's comfort.

Nixon, accompanied by his family, Haldeman, Ehrlichman and other senior staff went to Key Biscayne that Wednesday afternoon. When John Ehrlichman called me two days later and asked me to be his assistant, I asked him what I would be doing. He said, "I don't know." I asked what I would be paid, and again he said, "I don't know." It would be an embellishment to say here that my response was, "I'll take it," but it was close. However, I thought I'd better talk to my wife who was, I had learned in the year we married, fast becoming the senior partner of our firm. We accepted John's offer.

John was to be Counsel to the President, a title that was first given to Judge Samuel Rosenman, a political crony of Franklin Roosevelt's. The attorney general of the United States is the president's lawyer, but Roosevelt wanted to give a prestigious title to his pal and the office has been around ever since. As I understand it, the counsel in most administrations has been available for political and other forms of advice, a kind of *consigliore* of the White House mafia, as the words share a common root. John was involved in a wide variety of tasks and, by extension, so was I.

The counsel's office also handled the legal issues that came up with the president's personal property, approved proclamations (National Eat More Possum Month, etc.), reviewed requests for executive clemency, approved treaties for the president's signature, performed *pro forma* legal chores such as approving CAB air route changes which require, by statute, presidential concurrence, and reviewed legislation originating in the White House for legal sufficiency. Bud Krogh, Ed Morgan and Henry Cashin were the three attorneys John ultimately engaged to do the legal work. I found myself involved in everything else that came John's way. I even researched and drafted an Executive Order, when the lawyers were busy.

The transition offices were in the Hotel Pierre, a toney hostelry on Central Park South. I reported, quite frankly, still in a state of shock, to John on the Monday morning following the election. Our office was one room down from Nixon's (Haldeman was the buffer). Scarred steel government desks had been moved into rooms that, several days prior, had been equipped with fine wood furniture. Telephone men were still running cables and a general air of controlled confusion reigned throughout.

An incoming president has from the first week in November to the third week in January to get his get his organization together, to structure his personal staff, to appoint cabinet members and to start identifying the changes in the administrative policies that would represent his policies and politics. This is not what one would refer to as a long lead-time. It is a wonder that transitions between administrations are as smooth as they are. It is also an indication that the presidency does not have as much direct effect upon the life of the man on the street as one might think. Harry Truman said of his successor, "Poor Ike, he'll find out that being president isn't like the army. He'll sit there and he'll say, 'Do this! Do that!' And nothing will happen." He was largely correct.

Initially, most of John's time and, by definition, mine as well, was spent on personnel issues. Our first responsibility was the staffing of the new administration. Harry Fleming (the son of Arthur Fleming, Eisenhower's secretary of health, education and welfare) was appointed as a special assistant to the president in charge of political appointments. He was responsible to make suggestions to the president for all appointments, except for judicial nominees.

Harry reported to John and, in the early days of the transition and of the Administration, there was considerable interaction between our offices. At that time the president had the right to appoint some 2,000 people to *Policy and Supporting Positions*, jobs listed in the so called "Plum Book." Thousands of office seekers wrote to the newly elected president applying for these positions. Great stacks of mail were dumped in Ehrlichman's office every day for review and to cull out any that might warrant special attention. We sent the rest to Washington, where Harry Fleming had set up his personnel office.

We also created an unprecedented prime time television show which aired in December to introduce the Nixon Cabinet appointees. Several of these were old friends and several he needed to be introduced to, himself. Nixon proudly related to the national TV audience that these were men of "extra dimension," but it was apparent within the first year that such was not the case.

At the time, I had never thought about the difficulties in selecting a cabinet but, after watching their performance, observing their strengths and weaknesses, I recognized that it is not as easy as it looks. A president does not have in his circle of friends and acquaintances people with expertise in subjects as diverse as agriculture and defense, foreign policy and education. Even Nixon, who had been on the American political scene for more than 20 years and knew many important and highly qualified people, was handicapped in personnel selection. Further, just getting someone knowledgeable in the field is not enough. The cabinet officers are the top political appointees and they must be politically attuned as well.

How easy it must have been for the early presidents, when all they had to do was pick a secretary of state, secretary of war, secretary of the treasury and attorney general!

10. BIG JOHN'S PRESCIENCE

I suspect that a first visit to the White House, whether as a guest or an employee, is one of those events that stays with you throughout your life. In my case, an incident occurred that helped to sear my memory.

Shortly after the election, in late November 1968, the outgoing Johnson senior staff hosted a party for members of the Nixon transition team. It was held in the Navy Mess, a small restaurant in the basement of the West Wing of the White House. The Mess was started during World War II by President Roosevelt to provide meals for people on a short timeframe. The US Navy operated it like a ship's officer's wardroom. The décor at that time was plain; plaster walls hung with some original nautical art. (Oak paneling was added during Nixon's first term.) White-jacketed Filipino mess attendants provided service.

John Ehrlichman and I took the shuttle to Washington for the reception. We had been added to the motor pool list, so a car met us at National Airport and drove us to the White House. As the black Mercury sedan turned into West Executive Drive, the road between the White House and the Executive Office Building, I could hardly believe my good fortune. Here I was, just 31 years old, and a member of the White House staff.

The tables had been removed from the Mess to create room for a stand up cocktail party. There were some 20 members of the Johnson staff and about an equal number of Nixon personnel. After an interval, someone suggested that we introduce ourselves and we formed a sort of a circle around the room. I was standing beside Ehrlichman, who introduced himself as counsel to the president.

Then it was my turn. I stated that my title was staff assistant to the counsel. I then added, humorously, that I was the only non-attorney in the White House legal office.

At this point, John Mitchell, AKA "Big John," the future attorney general of the United States, piped up and said, "That's because they needed one honest man."

Ehrlichman added several other members to his legal staff prior to the inauguration including Bud Krogh and Ed Morgan, both attorneys. Later in 1969, John Dean replaced Ehrlichman as counsel to the president. Some years later, all of these individuals became caught up in Watergate, as did John Mitchell, himself. All were convicted of criminal behavior.

Mitchell's response to my innocuous comment took on a new meaning. I was, by default, "one honest man."

11. "Preserve, Protect and Defend"

Planning for the inauguration began before the election. That which the public perceives as The Inauguration, the swearing-in ceremony, is only the tip of the iceberg. There are numerous other fetes, fundraising events, shindigs and swell affairs, including: the Parade, the Presidential Gala, the Vice President's Reception, the reception for members of the cabinet, the Young Republicans Reception, the Governors' Reception, the Distinguished Ladies' Reception, the Inaugural Concert and of course, the Inaugural balls. With the exception of the ceremony at the Capitol, the Washington business community and the Republican Party organized most of these events. The US military is deeply involved in everything. They are the "institutional memory," the glue that holds it all together. They view the inauguration not as heralding the new president, but the commander in chief.

Each of these parties is of a scale and nature that would customarily entail months of planning and coordination. Since that much time was not available, the compensating factor was vast numbers of people, both paid staff and volunteers. This presented a problem in itself. Putting together an organization, defining authority and then controlling the activity defies management skills, but it gets done every four years, with varying degrees of success. John Ehrlichman and I were the White House staff involved in the process.

After my experience as an advance man, the logistics of even the largest of the events was understandable and manageable. What I had no experience in, and only some appreciation of, was that all of these events were by invitation only. This meant names, long lists of names. A telephone directory of a medium sized American city list of names. Moreover, all of the people named were important. An invitation to the events was not a mass fund raising solicitation. It was a recognition for money given or work performed. Supporters across the country had a propensity to get highly upset if they were not remembered and rewarded.

Today, when most people in business are computer literate, familiar with databases and sorting lists by criteria, an inauguration must seem like child's play. We had no such luxury in those pre-PC days. Fortunately, the Chairman of Inaugural festivities, J. Willard Marriott, had selected an excellent manager, Bob McCune, to ride herd over the masses of workers and organize the individual events. McCune was with Lockheed Aircraft, had considerable organizational experience, and was wise to the ways of Washington.

The actual inaugural ceremonies are a congressional function. It is the members of the House and Senate's show and they brook no intrusion. Early in December, John and I went to meet with the secretary to the republican members in a suite of magnificent offices in the Capitol. We were told in no uncertain terms that the ceremony was under congressional control and that the president would be allocated exactly 750 tickets. We learned that the incoming president could select only the other participants in his ceremony. We were also told a story about Lyndon Johnson who, needing more than his ticket allotment, called in his vice president, Hubert Humphrey. He stripped him of most of his 75 tickets, leaving the poor man with barely enough seats for his immediate family.

John and I watched the films of several recent inaugurations and were disenchanted by the number of participants in some of the ceremonies, unnecessary people who we felt detracted from the presidential address. Nixon apparently felt the same way and told us to use only the Reverend Billy Graham, an old friend of the Nixons, for the invocation and benediction. Several days later I got a call from Peter Flanigan, a senior staff member and a wealthy New York partner in Dillon Read, who wanted Cardinal Cushing to officiate, too. A day after that, a major contributor from Baltimore lobbied for the prelate from the Greek Orthodox Church. This was, predictably, followed by a request, again from a contributor, that a famous rabbi be included. Suddenly, we had three additional speakers to be inserted into the program. Neither John nor I thought this was a good idea and John talked with the president-elect about the problem. We did add Reverend Charles Ewbank Tucker, a Black minister, at Nixon's request. (Nixon made a serious effort to involve Blacks in his Administration. He had more minorities in senior positions than any previous administration in history.)

The use of the Mormon Tabernacle Choir was in consideration of J. Willard Marriott, a member of the Mormon faith. With the choir and two pastors, we felt we had enough religion. This was, however, my first lesson about Washington and how money exerted influence.

My specific assignment regarding the inaugural activities ended up making me responsible for the allocation of event tickets to the staff, family and "friends." Given the tight numbers, this was far from an innocuous task. So it was that Rosemary Woods, Nixon's personal secretary for some 20 years, and Murray Chotiner, a Nixon operative since his first congressional run, helped me with lists of names for the family and staff. (Chotiner was the one generally credited with the concept for the attack on the Democrat, Helen Gahagan Douglas. This earned Nixon his election to the senate from the state of California and at the same time the initial enmity of the liberal press.) The three of us spent a day filling brown envelopes with assorted tickets. We started with staff and family. Everyone wanted tickets to everything, but Chotiner and Woods allocated event tickets to each according to their merit and position in the firmament. The "friends" were another story. Great hordes of people had worked for, or with, Nixon over the years and all of them felt entitled to tickets. They were sure that "Dick," as many of them referred to the president-elect, would remember them and would want them to be taken care of.

I resolved the problem of supplying tickets to the legions of Nixon's "friends" (of whose existence we were unaware and who were not on other lists) by holding back roughly one third of the tickets we had available for distribution. These, I kept in a bureau drawer in my room at the Hilton. Only Chotiner, Woods and several other senior staff knew of this cache. When friends approached them for tickets and made a good case, showing they were truly deserving, they were sent to me.

I was unable to attend any of the receptions, myself, as I was kept busy answering knocks on the door from "old friends" from around the country seeking tickets to the gala, the Vice President's Reception, and other events. Connie was suffering with a strep throat and all this while she was in bed with the covers pulled up to her nose, as an endless procession of ticket-seekers trooped through our room looking for help. These included the President's Science Advisor, Dr. Lee du Bridge. He was a cabinet-level officer, but had been overlooked by everyone. It was bound to happen, and I had managed to keep a handful of the highly coveted reserved seats to the Inaugural ceremony for just such overlooked or forgotten persons.

By the morning of the 20th of January, I had dispensed all but a couple of the special stash of tickets. Connie and I were preparing to catch a staff bus to the Capitol when I heard a familiar tap at the door. I opened it and found not my typical customer, a joyful, well-heeled, dressed-to-the-nines Republican, but a little old man in a well-worn suit. He had come for his tickets, he explained, as he always had in the past. He had been General Eisenhower's jeep driver during the war. The "General" had later assured him that he would always be welcome at any public event in which he or Vice President Nixon were involved.

I gave him the last of the tickets and left for the lobby, happy to have been of service and to have kept the "General's" promise.

12. FBI FILES

Every new employee of the White House (and certain members of the departments and agencies, as required by their jobs) is subject to a background check called a "full field investigation" which is conducted by the Federal Bureau of Investigation. The individual is required to fill out a thick report listing every school he ever attended, the address of every home in which he lived, every employer, extensive financial information, tax returns, and more. The form also required the names of a number of references who, presumably, would place love of country over friendship and divulge derogatory information. It was a difficult form to complete and required time and careful attention, as well as access to old records, but most of us worked hard for accuracy. After all, who would dare give false information to the FBI?

I became aware of the potential for error in the FBI investigations in the first weeks of the transition. The office of the Counsel was the designated contact point for communications to and from the Federal Bureau of Investigation. It was also the reviewing office for the "full fields." One afternoon John Mitchell, the future attorney general, called me about a matter of some concern. He had gotten a call from J. Edgar Hoover, who passed on the information that an FBI investigation contained an allegation that a senior member of the White House Staff was a homosexual.

In 1968, homosexuality was not as accepted as it is today. A furor had developed in the press when Walter Jenkins, President Johnson's chief of staff, had been apprehended soliciting sex in the local YMCA. Moreover, there was a strong religious bent in the Nixon White House. I knew that being gay was unacceptable to Nixon, a Quaker, and to Ehrlichman, a devout Christian Scientist.

When I told John of the matter, his reaction was the same as mine. No way. John held a private conversation with the accused and asked him who might have said such a thing. A bitter ex-wife might. Jealous of her former husband's success, she was trying to sabotage his appointment. The FBI reports were raw information: no attempt had been made to verify anything. You could say anything about anybody and it would end up in an FBI file. Permanently.

Shortly after that incident, John told me that he had engaged Egil "Bud" Krogh, a young man from his former law firm, to be responsible for reviewing the FBI reports. I wouldn't have to deal with them anymore. This was fine with me. I had neither the time nor the desire to snoop into the details of the private lives of my associates.

Bud Krogh was a tall, attractive, sturdy fellow who had just gotten out of law school after serving in the Navy in an intelligence-related position. He had a family connection with John Ehrlichman in Seattle and was also a highly religious Christian Scientist. He obtained his law degree after his military service and the White House was, for all intents and purposes, his first employment. This was not unusual, as there was a distinct effort on the President's part to have a young staff in the White House. His great political adversary, John F. Kennedy, had been recognized and lauded for the youth and vigor of his White House organization. Nixon was determined to go Kennedy one better. (Lyndon Johnson, remarking on the political inexperience of the staff he inherited from Kennedy, is purported to have said that "he would be a lot happier if any of them had at least run for county sheriff").

There is a fine line between the desirable vigor of youth and the wisdom and judgment that can only come with age and experience. For the most part, the Nixon White House was judicious in finding a happy medium. The senior staff, Haldeman, Ehrlichman, Moynihan, Kissinger, *et al*, were in their 40s and most of the rest, who reported to the seniors, were in their 20s and 30s. I didn't complain. I was one of the youths.

The following memorandum shows the President's interest in the subject.

THE WHITE HOUSE

WASHINGTON

January 28, 1969

MEMORANDUM

FOR: MR. EHRLICHMAN

The President is very anxious to get the word out about the youth of the White House staff and suggests that we make a statistical survey of the present staff and see if we can't develop a major story on this subject.

H.R. Haldeman

CC:

Mr. Klein

Mr. Ziegler

President Johnson's management style was totally different from Nixon's. While Nixon normally wanted to deal with only the senior staff, Johnson usually wanted to talk personally with the individual involved. The telephone on Johnson's desk had 66 buttons on it, each a direct connection to a staff member, most of whom, to Johnson, must have seemed little more than kids. Actually, 64 buttons connected to staff. One was a signal to let his waiter know that he wanted a Fresca. The other button went to the men's room on the second floor. Johnson had once mashed the button for Califano, or some other denizen of the upper deck, only to be told that the gentleman in question was "down the hall." When President Johnson wanted to talk to someone, he wanted to talk. The next day, there were phones in the stalls.

Those phones were removed when Nixon became president. I was always glad that Nixon's style was different from Johnson's. There are times when you just don't want to speak with the President of the United States.

13. BUD KROGH

When John Ehrlichman placed Bud Krogh in charge of coordination with the FBI concerning the "full field investigations," he did so because Bud had all the right qualities for the job: intelligence, energy, honesty, concern for law and order, trustworthiness and the ability to keep a secret. These are all fine qualities, to be sure, and Bud had them in spades. But Ehrlichman missed one attribute.

There is an old expression in business, which simply states: "When seeking subordinates, look first, second and third for judgment. All other qualities can be bought by the bushel." Because Bud was a zealot in the mission with which he was charged, he lacked judgment in that area. In hiring Bud, Ehrlichman unwittingly sowed the seeds of his own destruction five years later.

For the transition office which I shared with Ehrlichman in the Hotel Pierre in New York City, I engaged a secretary from a temporary service. I'll call her Judy, though that was not her name. Judy turned out to be a brilliant addition to our small staff. Quickly, and without direction, she organized the office. Judy was an executive from the advertising world who had recently returned from a long European trip. She had taken the "temp" job till she located a more suitable position. She spoke a number of languages, possessed an impressive vocabulary and polished off a couple of books a week. She wrote with the skill of a professional writer. She was the only secretary I have ever had whom I trusted to transcribe my dictation and, if I was not available, review and sign the document. She was a whiz.

After a week of association with Judy, I talked to Ehrlichman about offering her a permanent position working for us in Washington. Ehrlichman agreed. When I asked her, Judy was thrilled. Being a senior secretary in the White House was far more appealing to her than being a Madison Avenue account executive.

Nixon was inaugurated on January 20, 1969. Bob Haldeman gave the entire staff four days off to move to Washington. Connie and I returned to our New York apartment, where she had already packed up everything but the furniture. We went to New Jersey, where my parents lived, said our goodbyes, and set out for Washington and our new life. Concurrently, Bud Krogh rented a U-Haul truck to transport the FBI "full fields" that were beginning to accumulate in a safe he had obtained. He didn't trust the General Services Administration, the Secret Service, or any other branch of the government for that matter, and drove the truck himself. This penchant for secrecy and security should have been a wake-up-call, but I figured that maybe Bud didn't have a big car and was using the truck as a convenient way to get himself and his stuff to Washington.

Monday morning, I arrived at the White House office I was to share with Bud. It was a large, walnut-paneled room with several desks, a couch and a refrigerator. Bud was waiting for me, with a serious look on his face. He closed the door (hardly necessary, as we were at the end of a hall and there was "nobody here but us chickens.") "I've had to fire Judy," he reported. And then, dropping his voice, he proceeded to explain that Judy, who was of Greek descent, had a brother who had been a member of the Communist Party in the 1930s. Bud felt that it was a conflict that he couldn't accept and that in the position of our secretary she, in his favored naval terminology, "could blow us out of the water" if she chose, as she would undoubtedly have access to our secrets. I was incredulous.

I called Judy and learned, between sobs, that she never knew about her older brother's association with communism. They were not close and she had not seen him in ten years. She was heartbroken. Moreover, she had more immediate problems, as she had spent the last of her money moving to Washington. Now she was in a strange city, without any contacts but me, without a job, and broke.

I appealed the matter to John. He was engaged with important affairs and had delegated personnel matters to Bud Krogh. He would not reverse Bud's decision. I was disappointed, but I couldn't argue with him. I was determined, at least, to help Judy with her financial problems.

I went to the White House Personnel Office, the permanent office that dealt with payroll and medical matters and met with the manager, a long time civil servant. I explained the problem and then told him I was going to sign Judy's time sheets for the next two weeks so that she would have the severance benefits to which she was morally, if not legally, entitled. I told him that this action was to remain strictly between the two of us and that if he had any objections, he had better raise them now.

You don't get to be permanent staff in the White House without being cooperative with the political staff. He agreed to participate in what must have been the criminal act of falsifying payroll time sheets. Judy got her two weeks pay and another job. (Three years later, after I left the White House, I was able to re-engage Judy as my secretary. When she eventually tired of the commute involved, I recommended her to a high-ranking US senator who had been a member of Nixon's staff. I told him that Judy was one of the few secretaries in Washington with a vocabulary as large as his.)

The extent of Bud's zeal became clearer several weeks later when he told me that he was going to have a wall constructed down the middle of our office in order to insure privacy when he read the FBI "full fields." This he proceeded to order, as well as a library-like carrel to prevent anyone from reading over his shoulder when he was engrossed in his work. He also had a digital lock installed, and an alarm system. Then he added bookshelves with a set of the Code of Federal Regulations and safes for the storage of his precious files. With all this, plus the reading carrel and his desk, his office was quite jammed. I, on the other hand, got the side with the windows and by default, the couch and the refrigerator. The only negative was that the chimney from the fireplace in the Oval Office was right outside my window. Given the President's propensity for burning fires, the windows could not be opened without smoking up the office. Still, on the whole, I was quite pleased with the trade.

A major issue in the 1968 campaign was "law and order." Nixon was a law and order president and had promised the electorate that he would pass legislation that improved the safety and security of the cities. When we arrived in Washington, John Ehrlichman was assigned the task of coming up with some proposals on how to accomplish the law and order objective. It was logical that this assignment go to Bud, with his Inspector Jauvet personality. Krogh promptly used it as an excuse to go to the Chief of the DC Police Department and get permission to ride around in a patrol car at night. He did this, ostensibly to observe problems firsthand. He was in his element and he loved it.

One day Bud asked me to join him, Ed Morgan, and Henry Cashin, both of whom had joined the Counsel's office as practicing attorneys, to look at some evidence that had been picked up in a raid on a pornography shop on 14th Street. This was Washington's red light district. It was late in the day and for some reason, I agreed. We took a White House car over to the Department of Justice where a trio of FBI agents met us. They proceeded to run films of the most disgusting pornographic acts I have ever seen. I was embarrassed and felt uncomfortable. Here were seven guys in blue suits sitting around a table at four in the afternoon watching dirty movies. There was absolute silence, which I sought to break with an attempt at humor by remarking; "Gee, those Democrats will do anything, won't they?" This was not well received by the agents, who were probably offended by my condemnation of their party. Clearly, the partisanship of the campaign was still with me.

To this day, I have the feeling that we were all "set up" and that the FBI has a record of my participation in the event in their files. Krogh had a different reaction. He was angry, and indignant at a legal system that permitted the public sale of films depicting such behavior. "Something has to be done about it." There was nothing half way about Krogh when it came to law and order.

In the summer of 1969, President Nixon requested that John Ehrlichman organize a Domestic Affairs Council similar to the National Security Council headed by Henry Kissinger. Bob Haldeman was to assume all of John's responsibilities not related to the duties of the Counsel. I would to go to work for Bob and a new Counsel was to be appointed. Thus, another opportunity was provided for Bud Krogh to err.

Bud's liaison with the Justice Department was conducted through John Dean. Dean was a fastidious dresser, angelic in appearance and studious in demeanor. He was also a great con artist and he ingratiated himself with Krogh. He found many opportunities to visit the White House, even though there was a regular messenger service between the two buildings. It was not uncommon to see him and Bud lunching in the Navy Mess in the ground floor of the White House. When the position of White House Counsel became available, Krogh recommended to Ehrlichman that John Dean get the job. Ehrlichman, who was under the pressure of far more important business, accepted Bud's suggestion.

In the following years I had only one occasion to deal with Dean. Shortly after his assumption of the counsel's duties, Julie Eisenhower phoned me. She had received union scale wages for appearing on some TV show and called me to determine how to handle the income. I, in turn, visited John Dean in his fancy office decorated with duck decoys. When I asked if he was a hunter, he said no, and asked my business. Perhaps he had heard that my wife and I were real outdoors people and hunters; but he had no desire to get into a conversation on ducks.

I explained Julie's question. He leaned back in his judge's chair, put his fingertips together, peered at me over his glasses in what was clearly a practiced pose and said, "I'll have to cogitate on it. I'll call Julie with my decision." I had an instant suspicion that John Dean was supercilious, phony, and untrustworthy. Time, of course, would tell. Dean and his wife Mo were not as they presented themselves on television to the public. Mo had a kinky reputation as a party girl and her "squeaky clean" look was as false as her husband's sanctimonious demeanor. He had been fired from a law firm for not exposing a personal conflict of interest and he had then lied about it to get a job at the Justice Department. John Dean was an affirmation of the reality in life that good-looking people have an advantage wherever they go.

Sometime after this incident, Bud Krogh had a final opportunity to demonstrate to me his lack of judgment in the comparatively narrow area of security matters. He was placed in charge of a newly formed unit at the White House. It was called "the plumbers," a reference to their mission, which was to stop leaks. When members of this group broke into the office of Daniel Ellsberg's psychiatrist, John Ehrlichman as Krogh's superior was ultimately blamed and he went to prison for it.

John Ehrlichman protested in vain that he had no prior knowledge of the event. Knowing Bud, I believe him.

14. NIGHT DUTY OFFICER

Shortly after we arrived at the White House, Bob Haldeman got the idea that there should be a "Night Duty Officer" similar to the "Charge of Quarters" or CQ common in the military. This individual would sit in the office of the president's appointments secretary, who was Dwight Chapin. His office was adjacent to the Oval Office and the Duty Officer was to arrive around 7:00 PM when Chapin left and remain on duty until the President retired for the evening. The officer was to answer the phone, respond to presidential requests and generally make himself useful.

I had served as a CQ when I was in basic training and remembered the experience unfavorably — a long night, chiefly spent trying to stay awake. However, this situation promised to be different. Imagine, the Charge of Quarters for the whole United States of America! The position sounded prestigious and had real potential for excitement. I have a very active imagination and a tendency to daydream when not fully occupied. I could see myself getting telephone calls of emergencies around the country and meeting with Nixon regarding their proper disposition. Power outage in Columbus? No problem. I'll get right on it and call you back. A mine disaster in West Virginia, saber rattling by Castro, riots in Africa — all of these events were in the realm of possibility. I began to eagerly anticipate my tour as Night Duty Officer.

A night duty officer roster was prepared and distributed to the staff members who were deemed eligible for this demanding and responsible position. I felt honored to have been selected for the second night. I went downstairs to visit with Chapin and get an orientation as to what I might expect.

Dwight, one of the nicest guys in the White House, was Nixon's personal aide (the Army term is "horse holder") in addition to his role as appointments secretary. He was a handsome fellow with impeccable grooming. As I am one whose hair always seemed on the verge of self-determined and uncontrolled disruption, I was particularly envious of Dwight. His scalp was covered with a black growth that was always in place. A reporter once described it as patent leather.

"Tell me, Dwight, what should I expect?"

Dwight said that I should let the president know that I would be just a few feet away in case he needed something and that I should try not to bother him. He said that the previous night, with John Brown on duty, had been quiet. He reminded me to keep a log of everything that I did, showed me where the sharp pencils and extra staples were kept, and left for home. Since the President was not in the Oval Office yet, I went to the Navy Mess for a quick supper and returned shortly to my duty post.

Nixon, though he ate lunch at his desk, usually went back to the Residence and the Family Quarters for dinner, after which he returned to his office to work. On my duty night, shortly after the President arrived, I had let him know of my availability. Then the phone rang. I grabbed the receiver and spoke: "President Nixon's office," only to hear a familiar voice say, "I'm on this line, Charles." Clearly, I had not been fast enough. The President had answered his own phone. I resolved to do better, and put aside my reading material.

The phone rang again. With what I thought was a lightning response, I again identified the office as being that of President Nixon. However, again the President had beat me to it. He must have had the receiver in his hand. This time the President advised me that I should not answer the telephone, that he was placing calls through the switchboard. "Get me Senator so and so." The switchboard was sending new calls through as he was finishing with the previous call.

My first night as Night Duty Officer was a bust. The President continued to receive telephone calls, which I continued to ignore. At 11:00 PM or thereabouts, he returned to the Family Quarters. I went to my own home, not having been invited to stay over in the Lincoln Bedroom in appreciation for my late work and fine advice.

After several weeks, the Night Duty Officer program was abandoned.

15. Haldeman and Ehrlichman

When Bud Krogh fired "Judy," John Ehrlichman hired Senator Roman Hruska's daughter, Jana, as his secretary. Clearly, there were politics at work, but Jana was an outstanding secretary and worthy of the job in her own right.

Rosemary Woods, President Nixon's longtime secretary, wanted me to hire her friend "Bunny," who had been the quick and loyal secretary to President Herbert Hoover. I declined the honor, as I did not think I would measure up in a comparison with Hoover, who had been an extraordinarily bright civil engineer and public servant. Unmitigated brilliance in the field of thinking was not my long suit.I chose two other, much younger, women. One, Stephanie Wilson, I recommended to my wife when she arrived in the fall of 1969. The other, Donna Van Arsdale, the smart, blonde, leggy sister of a high school classmate and former District of Columbia "Young Republican of the Year," added a touch of class to the office. All three of these women were intelligent, hard working, resourceful and serious.

It was due to the last characteristic that I was surprised one day by peals of feminine laughter emanating from the area in front of my office.

I stuck my head out of my room and enquired about the reason for the merriment. It seems Jana had just transcribed some dictation that John had dictated on recording tape and left in her in-box. She had just shared it with the other ladies:

THE WHITE HOUSE

WASHINGTON

57

MEMORANDUM   April 29, 1969

To: Larry Higby
From: John Ehrlichman

I have birds on my curtains.

I think I would like curtains without birds.

How do I get curtains without birds?

Perhaps there are people in the building who would like bird-curtains.

They would also be nice for a recreation room.

However, I think for an office like this, good old plain curtains would be nicer than bird-curtains.

And less busy.

Would it be all right if I took the bird-curtains down and sent them to you?

I look forward to talking to the curtain lady as soon as you send her.

The sooner the better.

I wish I had a terrace.

If Harry Robins "Bob" Haldeman were to write such a memo, it would probably have looked something like this:

THE WHITE HOUSE
WASHINGTON

MEMORANDUM   April 29, 1969
To: White House Interior Decorator

Re: Curtains

I do not like the curtains in my office; they are a print with birds. I would like them replaced with plain blue curtains by next Thursday. Coordinate the replacement with Larry Higby.

H.R. HALDEMAN

Tweedledum and Tweedledee; Haldeman and Ehrlichman — some of the press stories during the Nixon period in the White House gave the impression that Nixon's "praetorian guard" were the Germanic version of Lewis Carroll's famous twins. But, as the curtain memos indicate, they were quite different characters. There were, however, some similarities besides the German surnames.

Both had attended UCLA and they had double-dated while in college. I recall reading somewhere that Bob was the campaign manager for Jean Ehrlichman, John's future wife, when she ran for student body president. John was a Christian Scientist. Bob became one, although I doubt on account of proselytizing by John. Neither used tobacco but they were not against others smoking in their presence. I smoked a pipe. Bob would drink a glass of wine; John would not. Neither "fooled around" nor had any tolerance for those who did. Both were Eagle Scouts and embodied all the qualities that honor entailed.

Each of them was extremely intelligent and absolutely dedicated to Richard Nixon. Both avoided the Washington social scene and turned down the dinners and parties to which they were routinely invited. John Ehrlichman was in our home once for dinner, Haldeman never — although, in fact, neither do I remember ever inviting him.

Haldeman, particularly, and Ehrlichman to a slightly lesser degree, kept themselves aloof and apart and discouraged familiar relationships. They did not go to luncheon with friends for casual reasons or have meals for social purposes. In this, as the following memoranda indicate, they were faithfully following the lead of their employer. Seventeen days before he was inaugurated, Nixon wrote the following:

January 3, 1969

MEMORANDUM

TO: John Ehrlichman

FROM:RN

In considering my schedule for the first six months after the Inauguration, I have concluded that some drastic changes in existing policy with regard to state visits as well as to customs covering White House dinners must be made if I am to have the time available which I consider absolutely essential to devote to major decisions which I must make in that period.

Unless we get ahold [*sic*] of the schedule now I will be swamped with state visits, the usual customary White House dinners for domestic purposes, not to mention the Congressional and Senatorial appointments which will be flooding us during that period. A memorandum from Bob Murphy on December 24 indicates that 15 visits of foreign dignitaries are tentatively scheduled for the first three months of the new administration, from March to June. By comparison, Eisenhower received only six foreign dignitaries in his first *six months* in office, Kennedy 18 and Johnson 21. In other words, if we continue at the pace suggested we will have 30 in our first six months. I am enclosing the December 24 Murphy memo with the backup information supporting the requests for including these visitors in the schedule.

Nixon, once he got something in his mind, continued to think about it. New thoughts would bubble to the surface. The day after the above memorandum, he dictated the following:

January 4, 1969

MEMORANDUM

TO: John Ehrlichman

FROM: RN

I had a talk with Haldeman with regard to my own schedule after January 20. Presently, I am planning to get to the office fairly early and stay without a break until five o'clock. I am going to avoid lunches which take my time wherever possible. At 5 o'clock I will take off for a quick swim and possibly a rub down and will be available for receptions around 6:30.

For guidance in my schedule planning, if it is determined that a meal is necessary I think the best one to plan is breakfast. If, for example, we have a group of Congressmen who have to come in have them for breakfast at 8 o'clock and try to get them out of there by 9:30 at the very latest. Lunch takes two times as much time and dinner takes three times as much time. Consequently, we will save time if we can schedule breakfasts.

I am not keen on having Congressmen and Senators and others in for cocktails. I know many of them like this, but I am not sure this is the best way to do business with them. Where at all possible the cocktail drill should be avoided. If one is scheduled, it should never be scheduled before 6:30. This will give me an hour for the meeting and will leave an hour before the formal dinner if we have one. As far as formal dinners are concerned, I want them to start around 8:30 rather than 8:00. This will reduce the amount of time I will have to be there.

Under the circumstances, I have decided that the following procedure will be in order, regardless of whether the visitor is a head of state or head of government and regardless of whether the visit is described as a state visit, an official visit or a private visit.

1. I shall always be willing to have a talk with any visitor who is a head of government or head of state.

2. Where the visitor is a head of state I will have a dinner for him.

3. Where the visitor is a head of government I will have either a dinner or lunch for him, depending upon the recommendation made by State.

Even where the visit is a so-called private one, I will be willing to have a lunch if State recommends it.

But under *no* circumstances, regardless of the character of the visit, will I go to a return dinner or luncheon or reception of any kind which is put on by a foreign visitor. I realize this will break some china at State, but is time to make this shift in policy now and to carry it out in the future. This decision, incidentally, is not subject to further discussion. I have made up my mind and I have considered all the factors involved.

Even if I limit myself in this way the burden will be enormous. Johnson told me that he had exactly 200 visits by foreign dignitaries during his 5 years as President. This means that at the same pace I will have 400 occasions in which I will have to spend a miserable three hours in an evening, or two and a half hours at lunch, entertaining some foreign visitor. I realize this is necessary from a protocol standpoint, but at least we can knock off the tradition of the President going to return dinners, luncheons or receptions which simply doubles the load. In fact, my decision in this respect goes even further. I do not intend to attend any function given by a foreign embassy outside the White House during the time I am in office. If there is a meeting of the OAS or a meeting of the United Nations or a meeting of NATO or something of that character I will, of course, attend. But as far as single embassy's are concerned, I will not attend.

I have discussed this in preliminary form with Bill Rogers [Secretary of State] and I believe he will agree with this decision. The problem he will have, of course, is to see that his boys down the line don't get ulcers trying to implement it.

Wherever it is possible to get a foreign visitor to settle for a good hour or two talk on substantive issues instead of putting me through the agony of a dinner or luncheon I will gladly make the exchange. I realize, of course, that this will generally not be possible since the courtesy of a White House dinner is now expected by all foreign visitors.

With further reference to my schedule, I do not want to have the usual dinners which the President gives for the Vice-President, for the Supreme Court, for the Cabinet, etc. I would suggest that you see what these dinners are and establish the new policy immediately. I will take care of the Supreme Court, the Vice-President and the Cabinet officers by inviting them to the dinners I will necessarily have to give for foreign heads of state.

With regard to Congressmen and Senators, I think it is essential that you have a talk with Bryce Harlow [Chief of Congressional Relations] and set up some sort of priority with him immediately. It will not be possible for me to have individual meetings with individual Senators or Congressmen — except for those in leadership positions or Chairmen of key committees. That means the likes of Jack Miller, Javits, Allot, et al., can be seen only when they are part of a larger group. In addition, I prefer that such meetings be in the office for a period of time rather than for a meal or for drinks at the White House. Only when Bryce believes that drinks or a meal are absolutely essential to get the work done should such affairs be scheduled. The thing to do is to simply tell Congressmen and Senators that I prefer to talk substantive business and lay it on that way. I think most of them will be complimented if it is presented it to them that way. The way to handle them as far as White House dinners and luncheons are concerned, again, is to include them as guests at the dinners and luncheons for foreign dignitaries. Incidentally, where dinners and luncheons for foreign dignitaries are scheduled, it is probably best to include wives, unless it is absolutely clear that some substantive talk of value might take place after the dinner.

With regard to both luncheons and dinners, I want the number of courses held to an absolute minimum. Make the meals very good, but very short.

With such explicit direction as to the value of meals and parties as a means of contributing to the benefit of the Presidency, it is little wonder that neither Bob Haldeman nor John Ehrlichman became social butterflies on the Washington party circuit.

I have never reported to anyone quite so enigmatic as John Ehrlichman. His bushy eyebrows seemed independently controlled. He could raise, curl, lower or distort either of them at will. It was always an experience to give him a memo to read and then sit and watch his face go through plastic movements, occasionally peering over the top of his glasses while hoisting one eyebrow or the other in accordance with his unknown and indecipherable reactions. With all of this facial gesticulation, the only reliable key to his thoughts was his voice. John Ehrlichman had a very highly developed and sophisticated sense of humor that was always demonstrated by his voice. Like the poker-playing dog that invariably wagged his tail when he got a good hand, John's mirth could not be kept from his vocal chords. His voice took on a lilt, a softness, and a pitch that was always a sure give away when he was pleased.

John was also very creative, as well as something of a wit He was a fine writer; the author of three books, one of which, *The China Card*, is about as good a story of international political intrigue as can be found. He was a modestly competent sketch artist and his doodles drawn during cabinet meetings, while seated in the ring of chairs away from the table and against the wall, are classics.

Bob Haldeman, in contrast, left no doubt about where he stood. He pursed his lips, wiped any semblance of a smile from his face, and put on his sternest visage and barked when upset. The problem was, that was the countenance he wore most of the time. He always looked stern and unsmiling; that was the image he wanted to project as the president's chief of staff.

Connie and I had dinner in Los Angeles with Bob and his wife Joanne after he left the White House and before he was incarcerated for perjury and conspiracy, his share of Watergate. I observed a different Bob Haldeman, then. Later, too, when I visited Bob at the Federal Correctional Institution (FCI) Lompoc, California, I realized that his stern look and unapproachable bearing were part of a practiced persona. While still an *homme serieux*, he was much more casual and approachable when out of office and not serving and protecting Richard Nixon. He had even let his military crew cut with "white sidewalls" grow out to a normal, short hairstyle.

Unlike Ehrlichman, Bob did not have a spontaneous and free flowing sense of humor. It never would have occurred to him to write the curtain memo in a style other than that which I attributed to him. (On the other hand, I could never have anticipated John Ehrlichman's "bird curtain" memo, either.)

Haldeman was a stern taskmaster. His goal was an error-free environment and he did not appreciate nor accept sloppy work. He usually had at least one critical comment on every proposal submitted to him and would send them back to the author with a large handwritten "NO!" beside the offending paragraph. The following memorandum, with his neatly written comment, "you're absolutely right," was returned to me. It was the equivalent of getting an A+ in a college physics exam.

THE WHITE HOUSE

WASHINGTON

May 4, 1970

MEMORANDUM

FOR: H. R. HALDEMAN

FROM: C. E. STUART

RE: President's Speech

The President's use of a map of Cambodia and South Vietnam the other night was excellent. Television is a visual medium and exhibits can greatly enhance the effect of a delivered speech. Not only maps, but charts and graphs should be considered for future speeches.

It was best that the President did not use a pointer. Such would have made the President appear to be a lecturer or military briefer.

The television crews were deficient in their coverage of the President's use of the map and in his movement from the desk to map. It seemed awkward for the President to get up from, and return to, his seat. Perhaps, in the future, graphics could be placed on an easel at the side of his desk so that he could lean over and make his points without leaving his chair.

Of the two, Bob Haldeman was the more vilified by the press during his White House years. His remoteness and inapproachability were an anathema to them. However, he was not avoiding them with disdain, as many claimed. He was just a very focused, very smart, very hard-working man who devoted himself to the care of Richard Nixon. Many in Washington accused him of being the typical political aide who enjoyed exercising the levers of power. In reality, he seemed to appreciate full well Goethe's story of *The Sorcerer's Apprentice*. He was, to my observation, very careful to see that his actions and person were always subservient to Nixon's. Indeed, with the new White House staff together at a breakfast during the Inaugural week, he lectured us about our future behavior and reminded us that we weren't there to tell the President what to do. We were there to do what the President wanted. He also read to us from the writings of a Welshman, Tom Jones, who had been the private secretary to three British prime ministers. Jones had proposed to President Roosevelt that he needed one key aide: "A man possessed of high competence, great physical vigor and a passion for anonymity." Clearly, Haldeman saw himself as the embodiment of these characteristics and hoped that he would inspire others by his example. In this effort he was largely unsuccessful as, alas, among the senior aides only John Ehrlichman was an obedient and dutiful disciple. Henry Kissinger qualified only on the "high competence" requirement. On the other hand, all of us who worked for Bob tried to win his approval by emulating the master.

The Washington establishment does not understand a desire to remain anonymous. Such behavior is contrary to the laws of the nature; the average politician, senior bureaucrat and public figure of any consequence cannot afford it. To be unknown is to be without power. Power is the Holy Grail in the District of Columbia.

H.R. Haldeman was a very intense individual. He was solely concerned with the well being of Richard Nixon and the smooth operation of the White House. His job, as he saw it, was not to interfere in policy in any way. That was not his area of responsibility. Policy was somebody else's concern. Bob's job was to insure that all memos, presentations, papers and personal appearances were of such nature as to insure the efficient use of the President's time. He did this for a president who was very concerned about his schedule. Nixon wished to reserve his thoughts and energy for the important issues. Generally, Nixon was not one to get involved in the details unless it was a subject that interested him.

If a memo was too long, Bob ordered it reduced. If he didn't think a paper was worthy of the President's attention, he scrubbed it. More than anything else for which he was criticized, he did not permit meetings to take up Nixon's time. This stricture included some of the Cabinet members who constantly carped about "not being able to get past Haldeman to see the President." The fact is, much of the time, they had little of importance to discuss. If there were individuals with competing policy agendas, he tried to make sure that the competition did not reach the level of the President. In the case of the rivalry between the Secretary of State William Rogers and the National Security advisor Henry Kissinger, he was not entirely successful.

Without having worked in the White House, in any administration, it is difficult to imagine just how many people are constantly vying for the president's time and attention. To be able to drop the *bon mot*, "as I was saying to the President, yesterday," is, in the currency of Washington, solid gold. There has to be some control and Haldeman did an outstanding job of it. And furthermore, this control was often exercised at the behest of Nixon. Bob was willing to take public criticism for carrying out Nixon's instructions. Not only did he wish to be anonymous, he was selfless.

In recent presidencies, the position of chief of staff has been played quite differently. The chiefs are public figures in their own right. They even appear on the Sunday morning TV talk shows, hardly exhibiting a "passion for anonymity." This is as it should be. I believe that all senior appointed officials, including those on the president's staff, should be accessible to the press and the public. However, they should also retain a privileged relationship similar to that of an attorney and client, in order to protect the privacy of their communications with the President.

By contrast, the distance and remoteness that both Bob Haldeman and John Ehrlichman maintained from the official and social Washington ended up injuring them and the President. When Watergate erupted, there was no reservoir of good will, no understanding of their personalities, no base of friends on whom to call or who would volunteer support. Two fine men went to jail on what were effectively improper and untrue charges.

In addition, Haldeman could have required all new staff members joining after that first week to listen to a recording of his "behavior" speech. Many needed some guidance. I said as much to Bob later, while he was in prison. His reply follows:

> Dear Charles,
>
> Your letter was most interesting — with your views on Dean, Colson and Magruder. I have to admit that I missed on my judgments on a few people — but on Colson I had the same misgivings as you did — and brought him in solely on Bryce Harlow's urging. I then kept him against my better judgment primarily because of Larry's persuasive argument that he performed a great service for me and we could keep him under control.
>
> Magruder I thought could be handled and his ambitions directed productively. I still think this is the case — but at CRP he wasn't directed. Dean was just a mistake — but I didn't realize it till way too late.
>
> Other than those — and one or two others — I think we had a remarkably outstanding group and one of the great tragedies is that they have all gone separate ways. I had always harbored a secret desire to try to keep the best of the bunch together after the WH days. It would have been a formidable crew.
>
> All is well here. My very best to you and Connie.
>
> Bob

16. THE 5 O'CLOCK GROUP

The first members of a new White House staff are selected from the campaign staff. These are people who are known to the incoming president, have worked for him and are immediately available. Unfortunately, the skills that make for a good campaign operative may not be the skills needed to develop policy and govern the country. In fact, it is quite likely that many of the campaign staff will remain focused on that which they know best, campaigning. There is a fundamental desire to keep on promoting the candidate who has suddenly become the president. As president, there is an unlimited ability to draw crowds and make news beyond the wildest imagination of a candidate running for office.

The opportunities available for the president to appear publicly are virtually unlimited. He is called upon to speak at conventions, graduations, and large gatherings of every description. He is invited to receive awards, christen ships, break ground and attend events. Any group of people, large or small, will be delighted to have a visit from the president of the United States.

To this panoply of opportunities must be added suggestions from the staff to do things that will promote the presidency. Sometimes it seemed that everyone on the campaign staff had his own ideas about venues for the president's schedule. Clearly, there was a need for a group to be concerned with the president's time and image and to examine opportunities and make recommendations. Scheduling the president was a matter that required agreement and judgment on the part of a number of people. The 5 O'Clock Group was created for this purpose, the name taken from its twice weekly meetings at that hour.

The best public relations and political thinkers were placed together on a committee to review incoming opportunities and to make recommendations for President Nixon's consideration. Members of this group were: John Ehrlichman, Bill Safire, Pat Buchanan, Dwight Chapin, Jim Keogh, Len Garment, Herb Klein, Pat Buchanan, Ray Price, John Sears, Frank Shakespeare, Bud Wilkinson, Ron Ziegler, Harry Dent and myself. I was also the secretary to the group. I prepared the agendas and wrote up the recommendations that were sent to Haldeman. Nothing, and nobody got to Nixon without passing through Bob.

Many of the above-listed members quickly became too involved in other projects to regularly attend the Tuesday and Thursday meetings. Safire, Buchanan, Keogh, and Price, all speech writers, were usually present and became the hard core of the 5 O'Clock Group. The rest made about half the meetings. These four diverse individuals were a more than adequate representation of the political spectrum. They were also four completely different personality types. All had served with the 1968 campaign. Safire, Price and Buchanan had also been involved with Nixon in earlier years.

Pat Buchanan was the rock hard, right wing conservative that he remains today. I felt ideologically closer to Pat than any of the others. However, his aggressive style, bordering on pugnacious, made him hard to get to know. He held strong opinions on almost every issue and argued hard for them.

James Keogh was an older man, a past editor of *Time* magazine. A polite, soft spoken individual, he always represented reason. He was a political moderate and not an inflexible advocate of his views. He made suggestions. The rest of us could choose to accept them if we wished.

Ray Price was perhaps more conservative politically than Keogh, though certainly not as great an ideologue as Buchanan. He was a Nixon favorite and helped him with his memoirs. He was taciturn and distant, a man of few words. He was also gifted with excellent judgment.

Bill Safire was the intellectual of the group. He was also the historian and authored a work entitled *The New Federalist Papers*, which enjoyed high standing in the White House. Safire, alone among the members of the group, had actually been in public relations as a career. He had an uncanny sense of what was right, what would work and what should be done.

In addition to discussing various public relations opportunities, the 5 O'Clock Group responded to direct requests from Nixon. The President was concerned with his public image. He quite legitimately believed that he had received unfair treatment from the press in years past. He wanted to change that.

He was not the old "tricky Dick." He was a "new Nixon," and wanted to be sure that his public knew it.

Bill Safire wrote:

> There should be a readiness to admit that the Presidency is changing Richard Nixon; it has changed every sensitive man who ever held it. Not a metamorphosis, but the President is more relaxed and quietly confident than ever; less partisan; concerned with the sweep of history as well as the week's developments. Acknowledgment of this fact provides an escape hatch for those trapped in old anti-Nixon attitudes; because the man has changed, they can change their opinion without being forced to admit they were wrong before.

The following memorandum from Nixon seems prompted by his previous wounding from the press. He prescribes a treatment:

THE WHITE HOUSE

WASHINGTON

February 5, 1969

TO: John Ehrlichman

FROM:The President

To be passed on to the 5 O'Clock Group

I still have not had any progress report on what procedure has been set up to continue on some kind of basis the letters to the editor project and the calls to TV stations.

Two primary purposes would be served by establishing such a procedure. First, it gives a lot of people who were very active in the campaign a continuing responsibility which they would enjoy having. Second, it gives us what Kennedy had in abundance — a constant representation in letter to the editor columns and a very proper influence on the television commentators. As a starter, some letters thanking those who have written favorable things about the Administration might be in order and expressing agreement with the views they have indicated. In addition, individuals can express their own enthusiasm for the RN crime program in Washington, the RN conference technique and the Inaugural, and the general performance since the Inauguration. Later on, letters can be written taking on various columnists and editorialists when they jump on us unfairly.

I do not want a blunderbuss memorandum to go out to hundreds of people on this project, but a discreet and nevertheless effective Nixon network set up.

Give me a report.

Nixon's request was thoroughly analyzed by the 5 O' clock group. I sent the President the following memorandum expressing our conclusions:

THE WHITE HOUSE

WASHINGTON

MEMORANDUM

February 14, 1969

FOR: The President

FROM: Charles E. Stuart, Staff Assistant to the Counsel

            Secretary to the 5 O'Clock Club

RE: Your Memorandum of February 5, 1969 — Attached

The 5 O'Clock Group discussed at length your thoughts regarding the "letters to the editors" project.

The group recommends that this program not be implemented for the following reasons:

1. The establishment of the group and its coordination would be difficult to administrate.

2. An inherent danger exists in the possibility of the press learning of the existence of a claque-like organization.

3. It is not necessary. Nixon supporters are addressing editors without prompting. Letters to various editors are flowing in and are generally favorable. The example of the Evening Star's jesting comments on your early rising is a good one. A number of letters were written in your defense and the Editor published them with an apology (attached).

The 5 O'Clock Group recognizes the value in continuing public expression to the media, but does not believe it is in your best interests to solicit such commentary at this time.

My memorandum to the President was dated the 14th of February. Allowing a day to go to the staff secretariat, it would have arrived on Haldeman's desk on the 16th. On the 17th of February, John Ehrlichman received the following memorandum:

THE WHITE HOUSE

WASHINGTON

February 17, 1969

MEMORANDUM

FOR MR. EHRLICHMAN

I am not transmitting the attached to the President because I don't believe you would want it to go to him.

First of all, the report from the 5 O'Clock Group completely misses the point covered in the memorandum. He recognized the problems and clearly pointed out the necessity for a discreet but nevertheless effective network setup, and secondly they seemed to have overlooked the television side of the President's request.

After review, perhaps you will want to pass this material on to the President; but I urge you to give it some thought first because I think it fails to meet the problem in the way he wants it met.

H. R. HALDEMAN

The above memorandum is a classic illustration of Bob Haldeman's style. He did not disagree with the findings of the 5 O'Clock group; that was not his job. It was only his job to insure that the President's wishes were met, that his problems were addressed. No more, no less.

I do not remember what happened as a result of the Haldeman memo, but apparently the matter was unresolved. Two months later Nixon brought up similar request.

THE WHITE HOUSE

WASHINGTON

MEMORANDUM

March 11, 1969

TO: John Ehrlichman

FROM: The President

You will recall that on several occasions I have suggested the 5 O'Clock group might direct some of its activities toward the letter to the editor and call to television commentators and programs. I feel that such action might produce more in the way of hard achievement than discussions on the grand strategy as to when RN should appear and how many press conferences he should have, etc. I realize that some of the latter can be helpful and, of course, is necessary to maintain the morale of the group. From the standpoint of what such a group can really contribute it is important always to have in mind that everybody has some idea as to what the President can do and that the primary service of the President's associates is to see what they can do in his support beyond what he does himself.

In this connection, Paul Keyes has often spoken about the necessity to monitor television programs — not only the political programs but the entertainment programs on which there are deliberately negative comments which deserve some reaction on the part of our friends. One of the programs Paul suggested we watch was the Smothers Brothers. ... [This] Sunday night they had one sequence in which one said to the other that he found it difficult to find anything to laugh about — Vietnam, the cities, etc., but "Richard Nixon's solving those problems..." and "that's really funny."

The line didn't get a particularly good reaction from the television audience but beyond that it is the kind of line that should, particularly at this time, receive some calls and letters strenuously objecting to that kind of attack. I think it is not too late (you will probably be reading this memorandum on Tuesday morning) to have a few letters go to the producers of the program objecting to that kind of comment "particularly in view of the of the great public approval of RN's handling of foreign policy, etc. etc."

As I have pointed out ad infinitum this was automatic reaction on the part of Kennedy adherents and it should be an automatic reaction wherever we are concerned, both when we find something we want to approve and when we find something we want to disapprove.

Would you give me an indication as to what kind of program is being set up to handle particularly TV commentaries of this type as well as the letters to the editor approach. (The latter, of course, is not nearly as important.)

Nixon's introduction of Kennedy as an example to emulate was unachievable. Democratic presidents had "letter to the editor" writers in union halls across the nation. A simple phone call to the AFL/CIO headquarters, a block from the White House, could generate a barrage of letters to editors and calls to TV stations all across the country. The Republicans had no such PR weapon in their inventory.

Nixon also sent policy directives to the 5 O'Clock group. In the case of the following memorandum to Ehrlichman, Nixon is urging corrective action when misquoted. While this seems at variance with one of his core beliefs, "that you should never argue with a man who buys ink by the barrel," his observations are valid. A reading of the editorial is an insight into how newspaper reporters and editors worked and how an original error can be repeated so often it becomes accepted.

THE WHITE HOUSE

WASHINGTON

MEMORANDUM

February 17, 1969

TO: John Ehrlichman

FROM: The President

This shockingly smug "retraction" of a viciously false misquote in the marked editorial from the Sunday Washington Post indicates a problem I want you to zero in hard on with Herb Klein and the 5 O'Clock group. I know it is our general policy to let false statements by everyone from Pearson up to the Times go uncorrected on the ground that we can't get a retraction and that all we do is make the one who published the falsehood an even worse enemy.

I agree with this appraisal, but there is an even greater danger in allowing a false statement go by without having a correction demanded promptly so it is on the record.

Have all of the members of the 5 O'Clock group read this editorial and see what happens when this is the case.

The policy of this Administration, and this includes all Cabinet officers, should be to set the record straight whenever there is a misrepresentation. Usually the publication involved will not make the correction and if it does it will simply repeat the libel.

On the other hand, prompt action may result in the false statement not being used by others who are innocent with regard to its inaccuracy. Have Herb Klein follow up with the Cabinet officers, and Ziegler should handle wherever anything involves the White House or the White House staff.

F.Y.I. (*Washington Post* Editorial)

Elsewhere on this page today there is a letter from Mr. Fred L. Hartley, the president of the Union Oil Company, which moves us to return again, "For Your Information," to the workings, not to say folkways — of our trade. It is a letter almost identical to the one Mr. Hartley wrote the *Wall Street Journal*, protesting a misquotation which he says misrepresented his views ("maligned by a grossly inaccurate quotation") regarding the effects of a leaking oil well off the coast of Santa Barbara,

Calif. — a misrepresentation "particularly galling," as Mr. Hartley puts it, in view of the company's all out efforts to save bird and marine life. The story of the misquotation is the story of how the news business works. Or, as is sometimes the case, doesn't work.

The quote: "I'm amazed at the publicity for the loss of a few birds," originally appeared on February 6, in paragraph fourteen of a story on page 19 of the *New York Times*. It was an account by Mr. Warren Weaver of Mr. Hartley's testimony before the Senate Subcommittee on Air and Water Pollution. Mr. Weaver now understands the quotation to be incorrect, and explains that he left the hearing room for 20 minutes and on returning was given what in the trade is known as "a fill" by (the plot thickens) a correspondent for the *Christian Science Monitor*. It was on the basis of the "fill" that Mr. Weaver used the quote; a practice, as he accurately points out, "as old as time, but not very satisfactory."

Fred Hartley apparently did not get to page 19 of *The New York Times* that day, for there were no complaints from him or his office. In fact, quite the reverse. The following day, Friday, February 7, the *Wall Street Journal* picked up the Weaver quote in a front page story and supported it with the comment of an unnamed company official in San Diego, who appeared to have no doubts of its authenticity. "Lord, I wish he (Hartley) hadn't said that," the *Journal* quoted the company official as saying.

When a quotation appears in both the *Wall Street Journal* and *The New York Times* (it appeared in the *Times* again in a Weaver story in the Sunday news of the week in review), and is apparently confirmed by an associate of the quotee, and seems within the context of other remarks highly — how shall we say? — likely, the impulse is not to quibble. It is to pick it up and print it. It is not a good or a safe impulse, we agree. But it is exactly what happened, as events followed swiftly, one upon the other. David Brinkley picked up the quote on his television program, and *Time* magazine, whose checking service rivals the Vatican's, quoted the "blunt, short-tempered executive" as being amazed at the publicity for the loss of a few birds." *Time* added verisimilitude, as we say, with an exclusive quote of its own. It said Hartley described the whole ghastly business as "Mother Earth letting the oil come out."

So it came around, finally, to the editorial page of *The Washington Post*. We had been following these tidings, and on February 14 we weighed in with customary authority with what we hoped would be the definitive comment. And the quotation (or non-quotation) which had begun life eight days before in the fourteenth paragraph of a page 19 story in *The New York Times* wound up as a headline over an editorial in these columns: "The loss of a few birds."

In short, we erred.

So that it is the way it sometimes works. We are not pleased to report all this, still less proud, but we thought it had a certain interest. The true quotation, as transcribed by the Alderson Reporting Service, went like this: "Mr. Chairman, I would like to comment further here. I think we have to look at these problems relatively. I am always tremendously impressed at the publicity that the death of birds receives versus the loss of people in our country in this day and age..."

I am glad Nixon made this little story required reading for the 5 O'Clock group. But he did not go far enough. It should be required reading to graduate from high school. Every citizen should learn to question everything he or she reads. Just because it is in the newspaper does not make it so.

The 5 O'Clock Group remained active, twice a week, through the first quarter of 1969. By that time, all the members were fully engrossed in their own activities. There was greater confidence in individual judgment regarding the President's schedule. Dwight Chapin, Nixon's Appointments Secretary, continued to receive suggestions about activities that the President should undertake. I presume he asked other staff members for their advice. But, after the first 100 days, the President's appearances were mostly driven by political and policy requirements. Also, I suspect, the President had gotten the "letters to the editor" program out of his system.

The 5 O'Clock group was either disbanded or withered away; its purpose had been served.

Wide World

The ultimate campaign photo, some feel the best ever: presidential candidate Wendell Wilkie in 1940. The excitement of being part of such an enterprise is what makes people leave their jobs and become unpaid volunteers.

Nixon Library
Nixon in Chicago in 1968, nearly 30 years after Wilkie; the excitement is the same.

Photo by Author.
Ed Morgan, my friend, teacher and one of the all time great Nixon advance men.

Author Collection
The author in the Atlanta airport in 1968. The walkie-talkie has two uses: one to communicate, the other as a photo prop.

White House Photo
Bob Haldeman wore this look, or close to it, for the entire period in the White House

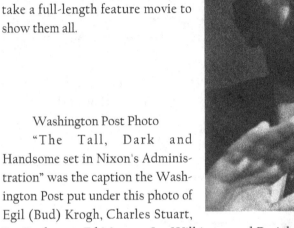

White House Photo
John Ehrlichman in one of his many facial configurations. It would take a full-length feature movie to show them all.

Washington Post Photo
"The Tall, Dark and Handsome set in Nixon's Administration" was the caption the Washington Post put under this photo of Egil (Bud) Krogh, Charles Stuart, Pat Buchanan, Ed Morgan, Jay Wilkinson and Dwight Chapin. Such dubious reporting probably contributed to the Post being placed on Nixon's enemy list. Of the six of us, only Buchanan, Wilkinson and I escaped going to jail because of Watergate.

Washington Post
The White House guard uniform that created a furor and gave rise to the accusation that Nxon wanted to be an "imperial president."

The Walt Kelly cartoon of a hyena-faced Spiro Agnew in a White House uniform jacket caused much concern among Republicans.

Photo by Author
Pat Nixon in her own custom Bangkok *klong* Boat.

Never Trust a Local

Photo by Author
The *klong* boat Mrs.
Nixon wanted to ride in.

Photo by Author
"Sock it to me"
was an expression
on a popular TV
show of the time.
Signs like this one in
Bangkok, Thailand,
don't just appear.
They are ordered up
by advance men, in
this case, Dan
Kingsley.

White House Photo
While we were in Bangkok, Nixon secretly slipped away to Vietnam to show support to the American combat troops.

White House Photo
Connie Stuart, in her role as Pat Nixon's Staff Director and Press Secretary.

White House Photo
Connie Stuart in her less familiar role as White House impresario. Here she discusses with the President plans for an Evening at the White House, one of the series of Nixon White House events featuring American performing artists.

Author Collection
After Connie was hired by Mrs. Nixon, we became the "other couple in the White House." This was deemed novel enough to warrant a cover story by the Sunday Supplement *Family Weekly*.

Author Collection With Julie and David Eisenhower in the pavilion of the USSR at the World Fair in Osaka, Japan. To Julie left are Ambassador and Mrs. Togo and Secret Service Agent Bill Duncan.

Author Collection
The White House Navy Mess regulars at 7:00 AM breakfast. Left to right: John Nidecker (Staff Assistant), Ken Belief (Senate Relations), USA Colonel Charles West, Charles Stuart (Staff Assistant), Lt. Commander Charles Larson (Naval Aide to the President), Maurice Mann (Deputy Director Bureau of the Budget), Andrew Rouse (Executive Director, the Ash Commission), Ollie Atkins (White House Photographer).

Author Collection
The author with
John Kilroy, head
of the Los Angeles
Olympic com-
mittee, King Con-
stantine and
Queen Frederica
of Greece, at IOC
meeting in
Amsterdam.

White House Photo
The White House is never
more beautiful than at
Christmas.

17. Advance Men and "Attitudes"

Because of the extreme difficulty in planning and achieving a first rate campaign advance, the successful advance men began to think of themselves as a "mission impossible" team. The good ones developed an "attitude" that nothing was too much, or too little, to do for Richard Nixon. Becoming "hard ball" players was encouraged by both Bob Haldeman and John Ehrlichman, both of whom were former advance men and thoroughly inculcated with "attitudes" of their own. Bob Haldeman once stapled a note on a stale dinner roll. He sent it to the pilot of Air Force One, a graphic complaint about its lack of freshness.

In his book, *The White House Years*, Henry Kissinger relates the story of an advance man who took it upon himself to order a redecoration of the office of Canadian Prime Minister Pierre Trudeau in order to have the furniture appear more flattering to Richard Nixon on TV. An indignant aide to Trudeau stopped him before he substituted blue couches for brown.

In the same chapter Kissinger notes that when John Ehrlichman, as tour director on Nixon's first European trip in February, 1969, "sought to prescribe a guest list for a dinner at 10 Downing Street, David Bruce, our ambassador in London, who had seen too much in a distinguished diplomatic career to be intimidated by a new administration, cabled: 'Surely the absurdity of telling the British Prime Minister whom he can invite to his own home for dinner requires no explanation.'" These are just several prime examples of misdirected loyalty, but that kind of behavior spread through the ranks.

I must confess, with more than some embarrassment, that I too fell victim to the advance man's syndrome on the European trip. John Ehrlichman had left me behind to run the office during the week he was in Europe. I was also to organize a triumphal return ceremony at Andrews Air Force Base. As a newcomer to government, I did not know that the Department of State thought that such ceremonies were entirely within their purview of responsibilities. State had assigned a man named Abell in the Protocol Office to the task. I recalled that Tyler Abell was Kennedy's chief of protocol and presumed that the Abell who contacted me was that man's father or brother. A Kennedy holdover!

When Abell called me to discuss what he was doing, I let him have it with both barrels. I told him that this was a White House function and that he had no business getting involved with the ceremony without first checking with the President's staff. He proceeded to inform me that it was customary to have representatives of the embassies of the countries visited and the Dean of the Diplomatic Corps (at that time the ambassador from Nicaragua, Sevilla-Sacasa) present to welcome the President on his return. I covered up my ignorance with more fulminations. I also left a very clear message that he could organize the diplomatic corps and that was all.

Nixon did not trust the Foreign Service Officers and the career diplomats of the Department of State. He considered them to be "striped-pants cookie pushers." Such ideas became imbedded in the psyche of members of the White House staff who were quick to attune themselves to the beliefs of the "boss" to a degree in excess of that in a typical hierarchal relationship.

Being a tough guy was one of the paths to success in the Nixon White House. This was epitomized by Charles "Chuck" Colson's memorable statement, "I would walk over my Grandmother's grave for Richard Nixon." Any White House is filled with people whose nature is not to hide their light under a bushel. Bryce Harlow, an uncommonly erudite man who was Nixon's first chief of congressional relations, had also served President Eisenhower in that capacity. He once told me that "all White Houses are snake pits." Colson was an extreme example. He had previously worked on Capitol Hill for Senator Saltonstall. Quite legitimately, he felt himself more politically experienced than many other members of the staff.

When Colson was hired, he was placed in the office adjoining mine in the Executive Office Building. The EOB is that grand imposing *beaux arts* building adjacent to the White House. Most of the White House staff have offices there. That is where I moved when I went to work for Bob Haldeman after John Ehrlichman became Assistant to the President for Domestic Affairs. Some of the rooms were arranged with a secretarial office between two executive offices, forming a three-room suite. The offices themselves were wonderful: big rooms with 14-foot ceilings and 10-foot doors made of mahogany with ornate brass hardware, emblazoned with the seal of the War Department, the State Department or the Navy Department. The building had been built in the 19th century to house all three departments. It was known as *State, War and Navy* until World War II, when the Pentagon was constructed.

The day that Colson moved in, I went over to his side of the suite and introduced myself. In the course of our conversation, Colson informed me that he was a former Marine and had fired "expert" with the M1911 .45 caliber pistol. As that information was unsolicited and of no possible use to me, I can only presume that he was trying to impress me with his masculinity. Unfortunately, as a large man, I seem to inspire that sort of concern from time to time, as similar things have happened on a number of occasions over the years. Once, at an after-hours drinking session while attending a national security seminar at the Navy War College, an alcohol-infused Marine officer commented, "I bet I've killed more people than you have." That was a safe bet; I had never killed anyone in my life and had no intention of doing so.

From time to time Nancy Woodford, my perky secretary, would feed me tidbits about some outrageous thing that our suitemate had said or done. I always advised her to just ignore the man whom I (correctly, as it turned out) considered to be a "loose cannon."

One Monday, I arrived at my office at about 7:45 AM, after my customary 7:00 breakfast in the Navy Mess, and found it had been cleared out. Colson had arranged to have my things moved to another office over the weekend. To say that I was aggravated would have been an understatement. I stormed over to his side, but he was not in. I set about locating my new office while thoughts of a pay phone and desk in the men's room swirled through my mind. When I located my new digs, I realized they were an upgrade: a bigger office with a private office for Nancy attached, on the front corridor, a few doors down from the President's working office. I was quite pleased with the new arrangement and decided not to make an issue out of it. But it was another insight into Charles Colson. The tough, former Marine who had fired expert with the .45, didn't have the courage or the courtesy to tell me that he needed my space for his new Deputy, Henry Cashin.

Cashin was a character I knew well. He was an advance man and had previously worked for Ehrlichman. I use the word "character" advisedly. He was smart, from a well-to-do family, expensively dressed at all times, including sus-

87

penders. He was on the short side but carried himself with a bit of a swagger. The slightly pugnacious look and the large cigar seemed incongruous but omnipresent additions to his boyish face. These added to a persona that was completed by his chosen form of association with the English language. Cashin was right out of a Damon Runyon short story. If he proposed going out and "blowing a Benje on shooters and groceries," he was suggesting an evening on the town, spending $100 (a Benjamin Franklin bill) on drinks and dinner.

Thirty years after I left the White House, my wife and I were in a posh old Washington men's club, guests of another couple. Looking around at the personalities in the room, Connie remarked that it looked like the kind of place where Henry Cashin would hang out. Two minutes later, Cashin appeared.

As is well known, during his Watergate-related incarceration Colson "got religion." He founded a prison ministry for those in similar circumstances. Like many others, I was skeptical but now, some 30 years later, I am convinced. And I feel he deserves considerable credit for his undertaking.

In recent years I have had an opportunity to listen to some of the "Nixon tapes," including several conversations with Charles Colson. Each of the participants in the conversation seems to be trying to "out tough" the other. I personally never heard Nixon swear or use foul language. Mrs. Nixon told Connie that she was shocked when the tapes began to come out, as she had never heard "Dick" use such words.

Practicing psychoanalysis without a license, I believe that President Nixon wanted to be respected as a tough man. As with some males, he used profanity to bolster that image. He was certainly intellectually tough, but needed reinforcement of the type that comes with big biceps, tattoos or swear words. At the gym, the men's locker room is often a laboratory for such behavior. Perfectly presentable young men who are well behaved on the gym floor resort to street language when in the locker room with other young men. For Nixon, the Oval Office was a place to flex muscles, a place to bond with other males and assert the pecking order.

Much has been written about Nixon's insecurity and social ineptitude. He was not the sort of man to whom casual conversation came easily. Dwight Chapin related a classic illustration of this characteristic in 1968.

Shortly after the election, the 22nd floor of the Hotel Pierre in New York, the location of Nixon's suite in the transition office, received a steady stream of high-level guests and well-wishers. One such visitor was Cardinal Francis Cushing, the Archbishop of New York. As Dwight told the story, Cushing was ushered into the presence of the man who was about to become president of the United States. After the usual pleasantries, there was sudden lapse in the conversation. As a guest, Cushing did not wish to establish the subject of conversation. Nixon did not know what to say. While he was looking around the room for inspiration, he spied a football, the game ball of the previous day's Giants game, which had been presented to him as a souvenir. Eureka!

The next president of the United States, the leader of the free world, grabbed the football, and thrust it at Cushing with the exclamation, "Here Cardinal, do you want to see my football?"

No wonder he and Charles Colson cursed when they got together.

18. POTPOURRI

No two days were the same. Every day when I went to work, something new would happen. The following is a collection of small incidents which will give some insight into the White House life of an aide to John Ehrlichman and Bob Haldeman.

***

On my second day on the job in the White House, Major Lanier of the White House Police called for an appointment. As our office was the liaison with the police force, I presumed the Major wanted to see me on some official business. That was not the case. The Major came into my office a little apologetically and explained that he didn't quite know how to proceed. It seemed that he did not like my parking my 1952 Dodge Military Ambulance (M-43) on West Executive Drive. I had modified this truck into a camping vehicle, complete with ambulance litter racks for bunks, cut-out windows and a dark green paint job. It ran well, functioned beautifully, but looked out of place next to the black Mercurys, Lincolns and Cadillacs that populated the Drive and the side entrance to the White House. In New York City, we hadn't needed a car and kept the truck for hunting trips and to go on the beach at the Hamptons.

I assured Lanier that I was in the process of purchasing a Corvette and the truck would be seen no more. And, except one day when there was deep snow, it never was.

***

Sometime in the spring of 1969, I got a call from a White House guard post. It was about a man named Hess who wished to visit with John Ehrlichman. The guard was apologetic. Mr. Hess did not have an appointment but he seemed important. Would I take the call and see him?

Mr. Hess turned out to be the son of Rudolf Hess, the deputy leader of the Nazi party. By good luck he had gotten hold of me, a military history buff, in all likelihood one of the few people in the White House who knew the history of his father.

Rudolf Hess was one of the tragic/comedic figures of World War II Germany. He was named deputy leader of the Hitler's National Socialist Workers Party (Nazi) as he had been around since 1920 and was the 16th member of the party. He was, by most accounts, considered harmless and a neurotic dupe. He was non-threatening, ambitious, but naïve. In 1941, without Hitler's knowledge, the story goes, he stole a plane and flew to the British Isles to attempt to privately negotiate a peace between the two countries. In England, a nation of eccentrics, he was considered a couple of sandwiches short of a picnic. After the war he was returned to Germany, found guilty at the Nuremberg trials of planning war crimes, and sentenced to life imprisonment. Hess and five other top Nazis with lesser sentences were confined to Spandau prison, with each of the four powers providing guards on one-month rotations.

After 20 years, the other prisoners had all been released, and there was a movement to have Hess released as well. The Russians, however, insisted that he serve out his life sentence. Until 1987, when he committed suicide, Rudolf Hess sat in Spandau, alone but watched over and cared for by army troops of the four powers.

Shortly after the other prisoners had been let go, Hess's son explained all of this to me and asked if Richard Nixon would get involved to help secure his father's release. I listened attentively. I had heard that it was our government's position that the Spandau operation should be closed down. However, at the end of our meeting, I told him that he needed to talk with the Department of State. They were the ones he would have to deal with, as it was a diplomatic problem. I didn't have to discuss the matter with John Ehrlichman. I could easily visualize the news stories. Any lead that had the words Nixon and Nazi in the same headline would be bad for a person's career!

***

The White House had two telephone switchboards. One was military. When you picked up the phone a crisp, young, polite, male voice said, "Signal." This was an operator from the Signal Corps working for the White House Communications Agency (WHCA). He would then connect you into any of the military bases or Camp David, or patch you into the White House radio network in the Washington area. If you did not know the number, or where the person you wished to speak with was located, or even the name of the person you were seeking, you went to the White House operators manning White House switchboard.

The White House operators are famous in Washington for their ability to find anyone, anywhere, anytime. If you want to call Madonna (and I certainly can't think of a reason to do so) or Bill's Bait Shop "somewhere on the West coast of Florida" or the President of France, just give the assignment to one of the cheerful, efficient operators. Most of the time, within a few minutes, she'll call you back with, "your party is on the line." Many people on leaving the White House have lamented that the thing they would miss most was those wonderful White House operators.

Nixon was President during difficult economic times. There was galloping inflation *and* a recession. No Republican president had ever imposed wage and price controls. Such action is not even in the Republican playbook. There was certainly controversy about the decision. That is probably why on June 18, 1970, the morning after Nixon's televised address announcing such controls, Bob Haldeman asked me to contact some leading businessmen to get their opinions. I put together a list of senior businessmen who were public figures, picked some names and gave them to a White House operator. Shortly thereafter, I was open for business.

In the course of the day I spoke to the following people:

Mr. Ingersoll, Chairman of Borg Warner

Mr.Charles Tillinghast, Chairman of TWA

Mr. Lon Worth, President of Lon Worth Crow Company

Mr. Stanley Goodman, President of May Department Stores

Mr. Williard Garvey, President of Garvey Industries

Mr. Malcolm Forbes, President of Forbes Magazine

Mr. Brown, President, Reynolds & Co. (NYSE)

Mr. Howard Morgans, President of Procter and Gamble

Mr. August Busch III, President, Anheuser Busch

Mr. Kemmon Willson, Chairman, Holiday Inns

Mr. C.W. Cook, Chairman, General Foods

I did not ask them where they were; that would have been gauche. It is probable they were not all in their offices. They might have been visiting their company's operation in East Timor, in a Board of Directors meeting, on vacation with their family or even with their girlfriend in some hideaway. Those crafty White House operators found them all.

When I got the individuals on the line, I told them: "The President has asked me to call you and get your thoughts on his new economic policy." I knew how to play the game.

Of course, when the operators were looking for them, they didn't say that Mr. Stuart was on the other end of the line, either. They always announced, "The White House is calling." They knew how to play the game, too.

I was able to write the following memo for Bob Haldeman:

THE WHITE HOUSE

WASHINGTON

MEMORANDUM FOR:H.R. HALDEMAN

FROM: CHARLES E. STUART

RE: Conversations with Business Leaders

    I spoke today with a dozen of the nation's leading businessmen and sought their opinions of the President's economic address to the nation.

    There was a remarkable unanimity of opinion:

    1. Most believed that absolute controls are intolerable and ineffective. Hardly anyone is willing to accept another O.P.A. operation.

    2. There seems to be a general feeling of doubt as to the President's ability to achieve success with his low-key approach. There is an apparent lack of faith in the responsiveness of labor and industry, but primarily labor, to presidential requests.

    3. Bearing in mind that the opinions represent strictly a management point of view, there is a universal willingness to place the blame for inflation at the door of labor. Many respondents gave examples of outrageous demands in their particular industry and spoke of the utter impossibility of getting cooperation from today's labor leaders.

    4. A majority believe that the President should take a more direct action and set guidelines, personally intervene in negotiations, bring public opinion to bear, and in general bring the full weight of the Presidency into the fray.

One observation about Nixon: I never felt uncomfortable reporting the truth, when it was bad news. The businessmen didn't think his controls would work, and didn't mind telling me so. I didn't mind passing that along.

***

President Nixon received an average of 35,000 pieces of mail a week. Generally, the majority of these letters were on a single subject. Frequently, the subject related to war, any war (there are always some dozen or more wars going on in the world at any given time), controversial statements or policies, or telling the President how much, or how little, the correspondent thought of him. The balance was second grade classes asking for a private tour of the White House, Scout troops sending invitations to their camporee, couples seeking cards on their 50th wedding anniversary, mayors requesting attendance at the centennial celebration of their community and Rotary clubs sending advice. Quite a mixed bag.

Everyone who writes the White House gets a response, most often a form letter. I suppose to a second grader a letter on White House stationery is impressive; but that doesn't explain all the adult mail. The president's correspondence office is a lively place.

I imagine everyone writes thinking that the president just MIGHT see his or her letter. Nixon did, in fact, get a sampling of the mail each week, as he wanted to read what the people in the country were saying. He also got a weekly mail analysis, showing so many thousand letters in favor of this or against that. Nixon got so many funny kid letters that we got Art Linkletter, host of the Art Linkletter Show and author of *Kids Say the Darndest Things*, to do a book of them.

In the Nixon years, the Correspondence Office was headed by a man detailed from the Department of State named Noble Melencamp. Noble was a very pleasant man and an excellent wordsmith, but occasionally he needed some input from the president's staff with regard to a particular letter. As I was a sort of "minister without portfolio," from time to time I was asked to assist in such correspondence. John Ehrlichman also got mail from the public, for which I drafted responses for his signature.

A word about presidential signatures. No president likes to admit using autopens, but they have been around for years. Also, presidents' secretaries are usually adept at signing their man's signature. I remember hearing that President Kennedy's secretary Evelyn Lincoln signed a high proportion of the Kennedy correspondence herself.

The Yiddish language has a number of words for which there are no English comparables. This is the reason why many New Yorkers occasionally insert Yiddish vocabulary into their conversation without any hesitation or discomfort. "Mischpucha" is such a word. It was once defined for me as "a friend so close he can come into your home without knocking or go to the refrigerator without asking."

That signed picture from a president that is so proudly displayed on your wall is probably the work of a third party, human or mechanical.

Unless, of course, you and the President happen to be *mischpucha*.

***

Presidents furnish the Oval Office to their own tastes. When we moved in the White House, Lyndon Johnson's custom-made TV set still occupied a prominent location. It had three screens and allowed him to watch ABC, NBC and CBS simultaneously. Johnson wanted to hear and see what the evening news shows were saying about him.

Nixon preferred not to watch TV directly. He did not have time to read the leading newspapers from around the country. Accordingly, a staffer named Mort Allin and several sleep-deprived assistants produced a daily news summary which was on the President's desk each morning when he arrived. It covered the major papers, the network news shows and digested the leading stories of the prior day. It also reviewed the editorial pages and sometimes human-interest features Allin thought would be of interest to Nixon.

It could have been an Allin summary; it could have been a letter from a friend in Texas or even a congressman; but somehow Nixon got hold of a story in the *Houston Post* about a GI returning from Vietnam. It seems the man was coming back home the following week and was trying to bring with him a little orphan girl whom he had befriended. He was prevented from doing this because of immigration policies.

While ulterior motives were often ascribed to Richard Nixon, his Quaker upbringing led him to quietly attempt to help people in need. Over the years, he and Mrs. Nixon helped a number of troubled people and families. Nixon asked John Ehrlichman if something could be done to help the GI and the little girl. Ehrlichman asked me to take care of it.

A few days later, I wrote the following memorandum:

THE WHITE HOUSE

Memorandum   March 24, 1969
FOR: John D. Ehrlichman
FROM: Charles E. Stuart
RE: Vietnamese Adoption

Last week Floyd Newton Hand, Jr., a GI from Houston, Texas arrived home with Nguyen Thi Thu, a four-year-old Vietnamese girl.

Hand had met the little girl at an orphanage in Hue and was trying, unsuccessfully, to bring her back to the United States. His lack of progress was reported in a feature article in the *Houston Post*. The *Post* noted that Hand was about to be rotated home and, unless he could get the necessary clearances, would be forced to leave Nguyen behind.

I talked to all the people in Texas and informed them of the President's interest and asked what he could do to help. The stumbling block seemed to be a visa.

After conversation, the State Department was convinced of the need to apply the rarely used "Stuart Waiver of Visa Doctrine." On the day before Hand was to return to Texas, the arrangements were completed.

All of the people in Texas, Hand, his family, their friendly lawyer etc., are sublimely happy and, to a man think this has all come about because of the President's direct intervention.

One can only hope they will remember the name of the reporter on the *Houston Post*.

I remember commenting to one of the local judges in Charles County, Maryland about the sadness and despair which seemed to be so much a part of his courtroom life; sentencing criminals to prison terms, families wailing. He concurred. He told me that the only happy events that took place in his courtroom were adoptions.

I think I understand how he feels.

***

Part of my job with Ehrlichman was to be alert to opportunities to reward Republicans. The Democratic Party had held the White House and the Congress for most of the previous twenty-four years. During this time they had, quite appropriately, weeded out Republicans from all kinds of patronage rewards. The following memorandum discusses the recapture of largesse administered by the Veterans Administration:

THE WHITE HOUSE

WASHINGTON

MEMORANDUM

March 20, 1969

FOR: John D. Ehrlichman
FROM: Charles E. Stuart
RE: Veterans Administration Patronage

I requested from the Veterans Administration, and received, an analytical breakdown of the $17 million which they dispensed to fee appraisers, fee attorneys and management brokers across the country.

The incumbent recipients of these "plums" are listed state by state, district by district, and town by town. Examination of a town with which I am familiar indicates that most of the firms are headed by known Democrats. Fees range from as low as $55, which would appear to be a single appraisal fee, to as high as eight or ten thousand dollars for active law firms or management brokers.

This is the kind of patronage which is really visible at the local level. Accordingly, I suggest that you direct Harry Dent and John Sears to contact all of the Republican State Chairman and develop a new list of attorneys, etc., which we will push at the VA. Because there are no regulations regarding the VA's selection of attorneys and appraisers, we should be able to accomplish a changeover very quickly. I think this should have priority.

Attached is a memorandum to Sears and Dent for your signature.

THE WHITE HOUSE

WASHINGTON

MEMORANDUM

March 11, 1969

FOR: Harry Dent
         John Sears
FROM: John D. Ehrlichman
RE: Veterans Administration - Patronage

Chuck Stuart has a breakdown of the $17 million dispensed by the Veterans Administration to local law firms, appraisers and management brokers.

It is presumed that the recipients of this money are Democrats.

Will you please work with Chuck to develop a list of Republican worthies who deserve this attention. I suggest you work with the state chairmen rather than with members of Congress.

You should give this your immediate attention.

Cynics may think this is another example of Nixon underhandedness and unfairness. But it is not so. The practice has existed since ancient times.

In 1831, a Democrat named William Learned Marcy was elected to the US Senate. In the following year, on the floor of that institution, he spoke in favor of the patronage system of President Martin van Buren. In the process he created a phrase that endures to this day. It puts official approval on the practice.

"To the victors belong the spoils."

***

In the musical comedy, *Damn Yankees*, the Devil sings a song entitled "*The Good Old Days.*" This little ditty includes such delightful phrases as "scalping the settlers was the latest craze" and "that glorious morn, Jack the Ripper was born." I understand his lament.

I miss the cold war. In the "good old days" we knew who the enemy was and where he was coming from. It was the 30 Russian divisions of T54 tanks rumbling through the Fulda Gap. It was us against the Russkies, each trying to outsmart each other. Not some civilian in the Third World with an improvised explosive device.

One cold war scandal had to do with the new US embassy in Moscow. Our government had constructed a new building in Moscow to replace the over-crowded Spasso House. However, when it was completed it was discovered that the Soviets had implanted so many microphones in the walls that the building would be unusable. The KGB had developed a small microphone that could be buried in plaster. Of course, all the plasterers that had been hired were Russian.

Another bugging incident in Moscow occurred when the Nixons were staying in the tsarist apartments in the Kremlin. Connie was traveling with the Nixons and at breakfast the first morning, Mrs. Nixon confided to her, pre-sumably *sotto voce* and with hand signals, that the room was probably bugged. The two of them determined that the ornate chandelier was a likely location for a small microphone. They decided to test their theory and observed in clear voices that it would be really wonderful if they could have some strawberries with their breakfast. Sure enough, the next morning, without any explanation, a plate of strawberries appeared. As the Russians were so adept at hiding microphones it was very difficult to be sure you were having a private conversation. We countered by creating "safe rooms" in the embassies in Warsaw Pact countries.

I first experienced a glass "safe room" in the US Embassy in Belgrade, Yugoslavia. The only absolutely safe preventative against bugging was to construct a room out of plate glass and suspend it in air, in a larger room. Curtains were then hung around the inside of the room to prevent the voices from vibrating the glass. A major drawback was that there could be no air conditioning system, as that would degrade the integrity of the effort.

When the Nixon advance team visited Belgrade, the Embassy staff insisted that we hold our meetings in the safe room. I don't know why we had to do this. We weren't discussing military secrets or plans to create a capitalistic republic in Kurdistan. It was just part of the game of "cold war." As we were there in the summer, the room quickly became very warm. In fact, it became hot. It also became very stuffy. The Russian spies (it is presumed that in every embassy, the cleaning people, drivers, low level clerks, and plumbers are spies) were probably amused at our discomfort as we discussed such top secret issues as who would participate in the arrival ceremony.

Of course, "People who live in glass houses shouldn't throw stones." After the Belgrade hothouse, I have a better piece of advice. "People who live in glass houses, shouldn't."

***

On the subject of cold war spying, we had a chance to get back at the Russians in Mexico. The President was meeting with Mexican President Echeverria in the resort city of Puerto Vallarta. During the whole time we were there a Russian spy ship, bristling with antennas, cruised back and forth about a mile off shore. This upset several of us and we decided to play a little joke on the Russians. We created a phony four digit cipher (such codes were common at that time, before "bursting" and computer generated codes) and made a phony radio broadcast. I don't remember the names and number sequences. It doesn't matter. It went something like this:

Sidewinder, Sidewinder, this is bellbottom. Confirming code date: 3/71.
4798 3612 3980 1416 8827 1911 8056 4950...

It was our turn to enjoy a laugh, imagining the efforts of some Russian code-breaker sweating away, trying to break our "unbreakable" nonsense code.

***

The streets in the old city of Puerto Vallerta are narrow, cobblestoned and twisty. They are not at all suitable for motorcades. A press bus blocks the whole street. And, as in Boston, the press, staff and President were spread out in a number of hotels.

Mrs. Nixon was going out to the countryside in the afternoon and her car could wait in front of her hotel. The press bus couldn't get close and was supposed to meet us at the corner. The buses were kept at a sort of motor pool in a field at the edge of town. They came and went as we needed them according to a pre-arranged schedule.

As the time came for departure, the press bus hadn't appeared. There was no communication to the field where the buses parked. I determined that I would have to go the mile or so out to the bus park and stir them up, myself. Problem: no taxis, no cars.

A milk truck, one of those old-style delivery trucks with a stand-up driver and sliding doors was rattling slowly down the street. I jumped in the open door and commandeered the vehicle. I don't know what the poor driver thought as I have barely enough Spanish to order drinks and dinner, but I pointed to myself and said, "*Casa Blanca, Estados Unidos Norte America*," and made motions to turn around and go in the opposite direction. As he was a passive little guy in a delivery man's suit and I was an excited large man in a jacket and tie, I think I may have intimidated him. We were running late. I kept urging more speed with the rest of my Spanish, "*pronto, pronto, mas pronto*." Whatever I said, it worked. The old milk wagon and its cargo shook, rattled and rolled. I was part of the cargo, and I hung on for dear life. When we got to the bus park, I woke the bus driver up, said "*Gracias*" to the milkman and gave him a couple of dollars.

I exchanged vehicles for the ride back. I certainly didn't want to be seen traveling around the resort town of Puerto Vallerta in a milk truck.

100

19. The White House Staff

The White House Staff, as an executive organization, did not really exist until the Administration of Franklin Roosevelt. Prior to his presidency the staff was composed of a few people who worked for the president in perfunctory roles and a couple of people in managerial positions.

Roosevelt brought in a series of people whose names became familiar to the public, such as Tommy Corcoran, Sam Rosenman, Rex Tugwell, Raymond Moley and, recently discredited for his role at Yalta, Harry Hopkins. Roosevelt had a number of ideas for programs in his "New Deal" and he used his White House Staff as advisors, critics and operators. None carried the title of "Chief of Staff." That would have to wait for Eisenhower who, with his military background, placed Sherman Adams in the role. However, Harry Hopkins exercised more authority than others in the Roosevelt group. After World War II started, he actually lived in the White House.

The Administration of Harry S. Truman saw an expansion of friends and cronies in the White House, but a diminution of people with power. Truman, like Eisenhower, preferred to let his cabinet secretaries run their departments with minimal direction. Regular cabinet meetings, with presidential oversight, were hallmarks of the fifteen years of Truman/Eisenhower.

There was some concern that Sherman Adams, Eisenhower's top staff man, had usurped too much power from "Ike." When Eisenhower had a heart attack, a popular joke portrayed one friend saying to another: "Wouldn't it be terrible if Ike died and Nixon had to run the country?" The friend retorted, "It would be worse if Sherman Adams died and Ike had to run the country." This seems to be

Democrat humor, but complaints about Adams were largely the same as those levied against Bob Haldeman. They were principally regarding scheduling and access, not related to policy.

The modern era of White House Staffs began with President John F. Kennedy. He apparently had little confidence in the Washington bureaucracy to operate quickly. In order to "get the country moving again," his electioneering promise, he assembled a group around himself who became dubbed the "New Frontiersmen." This included Arthur Schlesinger, Ted Sorenson, McGeorge Bundy, the "Irish Mafia" of Kenny O'Donnell and Larry O'Brian, and others. These men were essentially bright and largely unknown, characteristics that Kennedy's staff would share with Nixon's.

Kennedy's men, to a far greater degree than Roosevelt's of two decades earlier, were activists and assumed authority over the departments and agencies with regard to the creation and administration of policy.

When Nixon became President, there was a high degree of organization, due principally to the efforts of Bob Haldeman. Bob did not bill himself as the Chief of Staff, only as an Assistant to the President. However, as with much else in Washington, there was a difference between *de jure* and *de facto*. Haldeman was certainly the *de facto* Chief of Staff. He was the big dog. Like the Chief Justice of the Supreme Court, Haldeman was *primus inter pares* of the other Assistants to the President. He was a skilled organizer and director of people. I suspected that he drew boxes with connecting lines as a hobby.

Nixon, like Kennedy but for different reasons, had little faith in the Washington bureaucracy. He wanted a strong White House Staff to create policy and legislation. The primary example of this was his distrust of the Department of State and his reliance on Henry Kissinger and the National Security Council (NSC). To coordinate domestic policy, the President created a body similar to the NSC comprised of the heads of the departments and agencies that dealt with domestic policies and programs such as the Departments of Health Education and Welfare, Housing and Urban Development, Labor and others. John Ehrlichman was named Assistant to the President for Domestic Affairs and the head of this "Domestic Council." The formation of the council caused the cabinet secretaries of those departments to develop new policy initiatives at the request of the President rather than reacting to the entrenched bureaucracies in their agencies. Ehrlichman, of course assumed none of the operational aspects of their jobs. The secretaries continued in the less exciting role of "running the business."

In addition, Nixon envisioned the development of new domestic legislation coming from the White House staffs of two men for whom he had created the new title, Counselor to the President: Dr. Arthur Burns and Dr. Patrick Moynihan. Burns had been chairman of the Council of Economic Advisors in the Eisenhower Administration and was an aged, doctrinaire conservative. Moynihan was a Harvard professor who had become famous during his stint in the Department of Labor during the Kennedy Administration. He had written a controversial book about Blacks and the break up of their family life. Putting these two diverse men together and expecting them to develop and agree upon policy was worse than wishful thinking. It was the White House version of the gingham dog and the calico cat.

The President determined that these two opposites needed to be coordinated by the new Domestic Council, headed by John Ehrlichman. John would bring the differing factions together and encourage them to cooperate on the development of the best ideas and concepts that were being churned out by Burns and Moynihan. There was some criticism of Ehrlichman, an obscure zoning attorney from Seattle, as insufficiently experienced for the task. Nixon knew exactly what he was doing. He wanted someone who had no built in positions or opinions. He needed someone with a good mind who would sort through all of the options presented and take the best of the ideas to the President. He wanted, and he got, a Haldeman for policy.

Another reason Nixon elevated John Ehrlichman to be the assistant to the president for domestic affairs was his feeling that the departments were caught in the trap of inertia (which they were) and that he could not trust them. After years of Democratic staffing, he felt that middle management in the departments would thwart any new policy initiatives with which they disagreed. To a great degree, he was correct. There were constant problems of proposed policy changes leaking to the press from the departments.

When John was elevated to his new position, all of the non-legal things he was involved with went to Bob Haldeman. I went with them and moved to the Executive Office Building. The legal portion of the counsel to the president job went, as we know, to John Dean.

John needed an administrative assistant to help him keep track of his newly expanded empire and he brought in the son of his law partner, a young man who had just gotten out of the Army, Tod Hullin. Tod was a bright, handsome, energetic individual. An outstanding athlete, he had quarterbacked the Washington Huskies in the Rose Bowl three years earlier. (After Watergate, he joined the staff of Donald Rumsfeld at the Defense Department. Later, when Jimmy Carter defeated President Ford, Tod joined me in a real estate development company.)

There is a general misunderstanding of the difference between White House staff and the president's staff. The former includes a number of organizations in the Executive Office of the President, most of which are statutory. These included the Office of Telecommunications Policy, the Council of Economic Advisors, the National Security Council, the Office of Management and Budget, the Office of Science and Technology, and others. To these must be added the president's own organizational councils headed by his senior staff. In the Nixon years, some 2000 people considered themselves White House staff. Of these, approximately 5% were on the president's staff. (In January, 1971, there were just 120 names in the directory to the White House inter-office dial system.) Of those few on the president's staff, even fewer had any real contact with the president. They served their time in the trenches, doing important work but with little or no "face time."

There are also a large number of non-political members of the permanent White House staff. These range from the Correspondence Office, the people who answer the president's mail, to the social correspondence group of calligraphers who hand letter the invitations to special functions. Add in the medical staff, the Military Aides Office, the florists, the cooks and bakers, the housekeepers, the serving staff and the personnel office, all of whom are necessary to keep the place running smoothly, and you have a large crowd.

I once met Mr. Justice Antonin Scalia at the funeral of a mutual friend. During our conversation, we realized that we had both been in the Nixon White House at the same time. Scalia was the General Counsel of the Office of Telecommunications Policy, headed at the time by a man I did know, Clay Whitehead. However, I had no recollection of Scalia, nor he of me. The White House is a big institution.

It is difficult to pin down the exact size of the White House staff due to the practice of "detailing" people from the departments and agencies. Every president wishes to reduce the staff size of his predecessor and then ends up detailing people to work in the White House. Commonly, new members of the staff are hired and then put on someone else's payroll.

Starting at the top, with Nixon himself, there was an ongoing, distinct worship at the altar of the Protestant work ethic. Life was not supposed to be beer and skittles. It was supposed to be hard work. People who enjoyed themselves too much were suspect. Ten- and twelve-hour work days were the norm and carrying a bulging briefcase on trips was *de rigueur*, so that no moment of "down time" might go undisturbed. This work ethic was not carved in a stone tablet, nor were reminders sent round to anyone who failed to meet expectations. It was in the air. Bob and John set the example. The President resented anyone even suggesting that his weekends at Key Biscayne or Camp David or the weeks at San Clemente were devoted to rest and relaxation. Haldeman used the term "Western White House" to insure the proper interpretation and image of *Casa Pacifica*, the President's home at San Clemente, California, as a place of business. God forbid that anybody would think that Nixon was on vacation.

The emphasis on work was probably overdone. The public would not begrudge the President some time off, or taking a vacation every year. Nor would they know, or care, about the staff taking it a little easier and keeping something approaching normal hours. However, Haldeman, as a former advertising man, knew that image was as important as reality; he also seems to have lost the distinction between the two.

Both the President and Haldeman were apparently inspired by the photos and stories of President Kennedy and his staff, working long hours and keeping the nation safe with their on-job overtime. But, for every photo of the Oval Office at night, there was probably a picture of Hyannis Port in the day with the Kennedys having fun and taking a breather. Connie and I have many photos of the President and staff, yet there is only one showing any athletic activity: a photo of Connie and Ron Ziegler, the President's press secretary, and other staff playing a pick-up game of touch football on the beach in San Clemente.

President Nixon's staff was a crowd of serious-minded young men and women. There was no resemblance to the TV show *The West Wing*.

20. The Imperial President

Much has been made of Nixon's desire to be the "Imperial President," but while it is a catchy idea the case has not been made for this kind of a pejorative characterization.

As a scholarly man, Nixon was a student of the American presidency. He had read widely and deeply on the subject. He frequently included historical anecdotes in his off-the-cuff remarks as well as prepared speeches (in which case, one could never be sure whether the reference was Nixon's or the speech writer's). It was this sense of history that magnified the importance of the office to an almost sacred level. Had Nixon been a Catholic, his reverence for the office would have put it just below that of the Pope. The act of governing would have become the 8th Sacrament.

With this profound sense of honoring the office, and I stress the office, not the occupant, his public conduct in it was highly proscribed. He thought that the president should not be seen as an ordinary American and certainly not as a common man. Not as royalty, mind you, but not as a neighbor whom you would invite over for beer and pizza, either. He conducted himself accordingly. Here, the case becomes difficult.

Nixon's personality, character and very being were inclined toward the role that he was elected to play. There are no photographs of Nixon playing sports, in shorts and a tee shirt, like President Kennedy, or of Nixon hoisting his shirt to show his abdominal scar, like President Johnson. There was no insistence on walking in the Inaugural Parade or carrying his own luggage, like President Carter. There was no attempt at the bonhomie of a President Clinton.

There would certainly never have been a Clinton-like sex scandal, nor any choking on pretzels while watching TV. A president must conduct his life unaffected by, and above, the urges and physical desires of ordinary men. Nor was any of the above behavior in Nixon's nature.

Nixon strongly believed that great leaders exuded an aura, that they possessed a "leadership mystique." In his book *Leaders*, Nixon examines the lives of Winston Churchill, Charles de Gaulle, Douglas MacArthur, Konrad Adenauer, Nikita Khrushchev and Zhou Enlai as well as touching on many of a lower order of magnitude. He clearly believed these people all had a special quality or qualities (granted, ruthlessness was often part of the picture).

Charles de Gaulle, nicknamed "le Grande," was, in spite of his pomposity, very impressive to Richard Nixon. His bearing was that of a man of consequence. Nixon admired this quality and aspired to emulate it to the degree he could. While de Gaulle was 6' 4" tall, he carried himself as though he were 6' 7." Unfortunately, Nixon was 5' 11" and carried himself as though he was, well, 5' 11." There were, however, other qualities that could be adopted, such as formality of manner.

Nixon was naturally a formal person. This was apparent in his dress and the code that he installed at the White House. The following memorandum, written before he was inaugurated, expresses a concern with the dress for social functions and establishes a protocol.

MEMORANDUM

TO: EHRLICHMAN

FROM: RN

    With regard to protocol at White House dinners, I have decided that any dinner in the evening will be black tie, even where it is stag. Where women are present, the dinners will always be white tie. Business suit will be appropriate only for luncheons or afternoon receptions.

The men of the senior staff were dressed in suits and ties at all times, except for John Ehrlichman who, as a Westerner, sometimes exercised his right to appear in a blue blazer and slacks. (He also frequently appeared in the office in penny loafers, even with a suit. As a conservative Easterner, this offended my sartorial sensibilities, but I never said anything.) Finally, Patrick Moynihan, that great free spirit from Harvard, sometimes wandered around with his jacket off, tie loosened and in bedroom slippers, looking like the giant leprechaun that he was. However, I never heard that even he was so bold as to visit the Oval Office thus attired. For the most part the Nixon White House strongly resembled a convention of the American Bankers Association.

Nixon's formality in the White House was, in my opinion, quite correct. Excessive informality can be read as disrespect and denigrates the role of leadership. Hamilton Jordan, President Carter's chief of staff, once appeared in a wool flannel shirt and hiking boots in a photograph of a staff meeting in the Roosevelt Room.

The only problem with Nixon's formality was that he carried it too far. One "photo opportunity" (chance to photograph the president) caught him walking on the beach at San Clemente in black wing-tip shoes.

It was this desire to be properly and formally attired which led to one of Nixon's first public relations blunders. Bob Haldeman and John Ehrlichman, in their desire to show the presidency in the best light, allowed it to happen. In his second month in office Nixon took a quick trip overseas to meet a few European leaders. Discussing the trip afterwards, he told John Ehrlichman that he had been impressed by the guards in the various buildings where had been entertained, particularly in the Elysée Palace. The French, who always seemed to excel in social situations and settings, had security personnel in highly colorful uniforms and hats that were more like decorative helmets. He told John that the White House was the only place he knew of where the guards were in blue policemen's uniforms with guns on their belts, looking for all the world like traffic cops. He wanted something else, something better, something distinguished. John gave me the assignment to come up with some suggestions for uniforms.

I have personally always thought the dress of the Royal Canadian Mounted Police was pretty smart-looking. When I proposed something on that order, a bright crimson jacket and pants of a darker color, John said he wanted to show the President some choices rather than recommending just one. Also, discussions with the White House police suggested that the Sam Browne belts, an integral part of the RCMP uniforms, even in the break-away models, were deemed inappropriate for close security work in the event of some miscreant grabbing one and hanging on.

I sent my secretary, Stephanie Wilson, to the Library of Congress with instructions to get some of books with pictures of police and military uniforms of the past 100 years. Surely, I reasoned, there would be something that the President would find appealing.

Stephanie returned with an armload of large books with colored plates of uniforms. We went through them together and paper clipped pages with pictures of uniforms that we thought suitable. I gave these to John to discuss with the President. I did not find out about their selection until I read about it in the *Washington Post* on January 28, 1970.

The uniform they picked was right out of a Sigmund Romberg operetta, with a hat that was somewhere between a London Bobby's helmet and a German cavalry shako. The effect was ludicrous. The hats lasted one night and were never seen again. (I later heard that they were donated to a high school band, presumably in Alaska.) The jackets stayed a little longer before they were quietly withdrawn from circulation. However, Walt Kelly — as cutting a political artist as practiced at the time — adopted that jacket to a permanent place of status on a hyena-faced Spiro Agnew in all of his *Pogo* cartoons of the unfortunate vice president.

Some years later, when it was discovered that Agnew was accepting cash from Maryland road contractors and engineers as continuing payments for services he had performed as governor of Maryland, the hyena visage did not seem so out of place. Only the jacket remained inappropriate.

Ultimately, the White House guards adopted that most American of uniforms, a blue blazer with a breast pocket crest of the Seal of the President and gray flannel slacks. The weapons were in concealed shoulder holsters.

In the United States, it is the current occupant who defines the Office of the President, not its history. While taste, decorum and morality are important, the system is complex enough and secure enough to accept a wide variety of presidential personalities. As with a series of quality actors in the performance of a single role, there is no right or wrong, good or bad; only difference.

21. The Asian Advance

Richard Nixon, like most presidents, was concerned about his place in history. He envisioned a series of historic events to secure that position. In his early years as a congressman, senator and vice president he had been virulently anti-Soviet. His position on the Reds was impeccable. He could never be accused of being "soft on communism." Thus he believed that only he could be the first American president to meet with the leader of a communist nation behind the iron curtain. Unbeknownst to all but himself, Nixon had plans to be the first president to visit Moscow. He also aspired, ultimately, to visit the Chinese capital Beijing. China had been closed since 1949. Opening China up to the West would be the preeminent accomplishment of his presidency.

In 1947, during his first term in the congress, Nixon was one of the few Republicans who actively supported the Marshall Plan of the Truman Administration. His interests and thinking were global in scale, even then. He was on a committee that investigated the effectiveness of the Marshall Plan and he traveled widely in Europe. Most importantly, he met a series of young officials and junior officers who were destined to rise to leadership positions in their governments. As vice president, he substituted for the president on overseas trips. Eisenhower, after a lifetime of traveling in the military, relished the opportunity to be at home. Nixon took one trip of a length that would be unthinkable today, a 60-day fact-finding mission to Asia in 1952. In the years when he was out of office, from 1960 to 1968, he traveled extensively in Europe and Asia and kept up his contacts as a private citizen. One of the individuals he came to know was a Romanian strong man named Nicolae Ceausescu. If there was not affection, there was mutual respect. In fact, we were told that Ceausescu had predicted that Nixon would rise to become president of his country as early as 1960, the year Nixon lost to Kennedy.

Nixon was sworn in as the 38th president on January 20, 1969. In June of that year he arranged with Ceausescu to be invited for a state visit to Romania in August. At the time, Ceausescu was not seen as a great rogue operator like Tito of Yugoslavia. Romania was the only the Eastern European nation that refused to participate in Russia's brutal quelling of the Czechoslovakian uprising in 1968, and Bucharest tried to be more independent of its Moscow masters. Ceausescu undoubtedly felt that having Nixon break through the iron curtain to visit Romania would be good for his reputation as well as tweak the leadership of the Soviet Union. Just a few decades later, it is hard to imagine the cold war relationship with the Warsaw bloc. At the time, it was widely believed that the West inevitably would someday find itself at war with the Soviets. Visiting a communist country and bearding the lion in his den would certainly qualify as a "historic first" for Richard Nixon.

In July of 1969, John Whitaker, the secretary to the cabinet and a Nixon loyalist of several campaigns, asked me to be his deputy, as tour director of a trip to Asia which was planned for August. The trip was planned around a number of "historic firsts." It was to be the largest and longest presidential trip ever undertaken. It also included a rendezvous on an aircraft carrier with the Apollo 11 astronauts who were due to splash down in the Pacific near Johnson Island, and the unveiling of "The Nixon Doctrine," on Guam. These would be followed by visits to Manila, Jakarta, Bangkok, New Delhi, Lahore, Bucharest, and finally London. Nixon even planned to sneak into Vietnam for a secret visit to the US combat troops on a day that was supposed to be a resting period in Bangkok.

By any standard, this was an ambitious program. Nixon wanted to welcome the astronauts back to earth. They were *the* American heroes of that period. He also wanted announce "The Nixon Doctrine," a concept that essentially modified the ground rules of the South East Asia Treaty Organization. It posited that the US would provide training and equipment for Asian armies but would no longer, after Vietnam, introduce its own forces. At a time when the "domino effect" was still a major foreign policy concern, this change in commitment has to be explained to US allies in the area. Finally, Nixon was eager to enter into a new era of detente with Russia and the Eastern European countries. Romania was deemed the ideal place to start.

111

In thinking back about the concepts involved in detente, I must admit that I was not a big enough thinker to believe that Nixon could pull it off. I was of a generation of Americans raised on distrust of the Soviet Union and its client states. I was pleased and excited to be selected for the trip, but doubtful about the outcome. I wasn't even sure about the wisdom of trying to cozy up to the Warsaw Pact countries. I did not believe they could be trusted to honor their agreements. Detente was — to me and other conservatives — a dirty word.

In foreign countries, US presidents are feted and shown honors well beyond those that they receive at home. Other nations generally pull out all the stops when a president comes to town. Governments shut down for the day in order to turn out cheering throngs. Colorful honor guards on horses accompany motorcades. Overnight accommodations are in palaces, not Blair House. Every modern president has traveled extensively overseas, to a degree far beyond that required by foreign policy concerns. Never does a US president feel as powerful as when Air Force One drops out of the sky in some distant nation and the president exits the plane to a carefully planned arrival ceremony. However, all of this requires advancing. An enormous amount of advancing.

The advance team that assembled on West Executive Drive at 7:00 AM, one July morning, was impressive. There were about thirty young men, many of whom would be dropped off along the way and remain in their assigned country. They would coordinate the vast numbers of additional people who would be leaving Washington in the next two weeks. John Whitaker and I (and a few others) made the entire advance trip and a week later went off with the President. Eclipsing the record of the Jules Verne story, *Around the World in Eighty Days*, we circumnavigated the globe twice in less than a month.

Unless one has been part of presidential travel, and I mean *really* part of presidential travel, there is no way to imagine just how much effort is involved. It is not like calling Cook's Tours and buying tickets for a trip.

There was medical advance, Air Force advance, WHCA (White House Communications Agency) advance, Secret Service advance, baggage advance, State Department advance, press advance, helicopter advance, hotel advance and somewhere, unseen, but out there nevertheless, CIA advance. John Whitaker and I covered political advance. I was to put together a schedule for Mrs. Nixon and serve as Whitaker's deputy. John Whitaker was overall in charge of the trip, a kind of Supreme Allied Commander.

The bulk of the effort and greatest complexity had to do with communications. The president is required to be in constant connection with Washington.

The military aide who carries the nuclear targeting codes in a briefcase called the "football" is always just a few feet away from the president. As radio communication was deemed to be interruptible, backup landline telephones had to be available in every location where the President stayed or was out of his car. Each of the staff also required a Signal Corps telephone at his bedside. Other signal telephones were installed in offices and command post. This necessitated running miles of cable and installing switchboards in every country we visited. When I discussed this effort with the Army general in charge, he told me that the trip required 18 C-141s, the largest cargo plane available at the time, full of communications gear. Because nobody wanted to screw up with the President, there was a lot of redundancy. In Bangkok, we stayed at the Royal Palace where, walking around the grounds one evening, I found an Air Force generating system in operation. It was a huge diesel engine and generator rig mounted on a 40' tractor-trailer. Behind it, on another 40' trailer, was the back up system. And behind the back up system was a third identical trailer, the back up to the back up. There was no way that the officer in charge of providing electricity was going to have to explain to a board of inquiry why he failed his commander in chief by not providing power for his electric razor!

Another C-141 was devoted to helicopters. There was always a presidential UH-1 (Huey) in the air when the President was in his car, for emergency evacuation purposes. This required a helicopter advance team to make arrangements. Where were the choppers going to be based? Where were the crews to stay? How would the helicopters be secured and guarded? Where would they be refueled?

An additional C-141 was exclusively used by the Secret Service to move the cars and extra agents. It was simply called the "car plane." Presidents' cars have a lot of features not found in your average limousine. They are bullet proof, mine resistant, gas proof, equipped with "run flat" tires and stuffed with radio gear and Uzi sub machine guns. The Secret Service will not permit the president to ride in any other car. This created a little distress in India. On the advance trip, in a meeting at the US embassy, we were informed that Indian custom and pride would not permit Prime Minister Indira Gandhi to ride in any car but her own. The President would have to ride with her. There seemed to be an impasse. Then, some innovative foreign service officer suggested we give the President's car to the Indian Government, put Indian tags on it and then take it back when we left. There was a collective sigh of relief. I observed that such an action would make us "Indian givers," and there was a collective groan. However, it was a good idea and we did it.

The medical advance team checked out the local hospitals and medical staff and supplied a quantity of blood matching the President's type. If the medical facilities were found to be substandard, presumably a MASH unit would have been scrounged from someplace and flown in.

The baggage advance team was not just hiring porters to tote luggage. It was responsible for all of the personal baggage and equipment of the staff and press corps and insuring that it was delivered to the right hotel. The camera crews, of which there were many, generated a large number of black, look-alike cases full of expensive, fragile technology; they required special handling. On the Asian trip, there were approximately 1000 staff and press and other personnel to be accommodated at every stop.

If the requests advance men make on local campaign offices in the States often seemed overwhelming, the security and logistics demands of a presidential visitation must have left people shaking their heads in the countries we visited. Most of the officials probably hoped we left soon. Just imagine, coming in as a guest for two days and bringing your own telephone network!

I have never observed a newspaper story or TV feature exploring the size and cost of such operations. The White House press corps loves foreign travel, and have no incentive to reveal how costly it can be. Even though their employers pay their airfare by chartering planes, a presidential trip to some exotic country is always a good thing to break up the monotony of Washington. When articles about travel expense do appear, they are usually related to some minor official having to reimburse the government a modest sum for misuse of a military aircraft.

As this trip developed, it became more apparent how dependent the Office of the President is upon the military. The Army is in charge of the White House motor pool and keeping it stocked with polite, fresh-faced enlisted men as drivers. The Navy operates Camp David and is responsible to organize the social aides, those handsome junior officers of all the services who insure the color and efficiency of White House social events. The Marine Corps flies the presidential helicopters and the Air Force supplies the aircraft, from Air Force One down to the King Airs that were part of the fleet at the time. The president is, of course, the commander in chief of the armed forces. The services, with their traditions of taking care of their senior officers, held nothing back for the CINC, and this Asian journey was spectacular.

For the Asian advance we took a military bus to Andrews Air Force Base outside of Washington, DC and boarded the back-up aircraft to Air Force One. Any plane the President is on is technically Air Force One, but a specially-configured Boeing 707 with tail number 8970 was known as the back-up aircraft. It was President Kennedy's primary aircraft and *the* Air Force One until President Johnson got a new one.

When you climbed the stairs and went in at the nose of 8970, it seemed like any other 707 but as soon as you entered the difference was apparent and overwhelming. The cockpit was completely redesigned and included such additions as two separate GPS (Global Positioning Satellite) systems. Such systems are now commonplace but this was at a time when there were only a few such systems in the world and they were all military. Immediately on the right was the communications area with a six-foot long console jammed with equipment. The RO (Radio Operator) kept in contact with Andrews Air Force Base at all times, even when on the ground on the other side of the globe. The president has to stay in constant touch with the military commands around the world. Colonel Don Hughes, US Air Force, the military assistant to the president, tested this system by mistake by pushing a wrong button when we were over the Pacific. In 40 seconds a startled Hughes had all of the five CINCs (Commanders in Chief) on the line on a conference call. Considering the time differences involved, CINCPAC (Pacific) was in the middle of his day while CINCEUR (Europe) was asleep in his bed. This was quite a communication system.

Located throughout the aircraft were red telephones that connected to the radio operator. If you picked one up and asked for the White House, there was no hesitation, you got through. From all over the world, the signal was as loud and clear as though you were at your office in Washington.

Immediately aft of the communications center, the aisle became a narrow passage on the left side of the plane as you went by the president's bedroom and lavatory. Then it opened up into his meeting compartment with seating around the bulkheads for guests. An electrically elevated table served as a low cocktail table or a higher dining table. There was only one chair at the end of the table and it, too, was motor driven. There was no doubt about whose seat this was, although on this trip it was not off limits. We all enjoyed sitting in the president's chair.

In the next compartment was a conventional seating area with a number of seats followed by an airborne office with two desks, electric typewriters and a Xerox machine. The office compartment was usually staffed with yeoman, the military equivalent of a secretary. There were several permanent people in these positions. I have seen them typing away while a storm was throwing the aircraft around; they just sat at their desks and typed away.

After the office was another staff compartment, followed by seating for a small Secret Service detail and a press pool. When the president was aboard, there was an unwritten rule that you should not move forward from the compartment to which you were assigned. At opposite ends of the plane were large galleys in which Air Force stewards produced meals unlike any served on United Airlines. The back-up to Air Force One was quite a bird.

We landed at Travis AFB in California for refueling and then headed for Hawaii for an overnight stop before heading further West. My assigned seatmate on the trip, before we began dropping people off and could sit where we wished, was a Navy lt. commander named Charles (Chuck) R. Larson, the naval aide to the president. Each of the military services is represented in the White House. One of the service representatives is the military assistant to the president and the other three service representatives are called military aides. I had come to know Chuck when he helped me arrange a reception for the staff after our swearing-in by Chief Justice Earle Warren. The President wanted a punch and cookies party and the responsibility was passed down the line to me. I had no idea whom to talk to but someone suggested that I call a guy named Larson in the Military Aides Office. I did so and got Chuck, who was most efficient and helpful. These were enduring qualities with Larson. He went on to earn the four stars of an admiral and the position of CINCPAC (Commander in Chief, Pacific), arguably the fourth most important job in the military after chairman of the joint chiefs, army chief of staff and chief of naval operations.

22. THE DRAGON LADY

When I was a child, during the Second World War, one of my favorite comic strips was *Terry and the Pirates*. Like many cartoon characters of the time, Terry had gone to war. The creator, Milton Caniff, inserted buck-toothed, bespectacled, grinning Japs, as was the characterization at the time, plotting against the US of A. Terry always foiled their schemes but was less successful against his female *bête noire*, the Dragon Lady, who seemed to escape with regularity. As I grew older, I came to realize that this was not due to a lack of resolve on Terry's part. Caniff had invented a character he couldn't kill off, particularly after the war ended. Little did I suspect that, some 25 years later, I would encounter a real Dragon Lady.

As a World War II history buff, I had done considerable reading about the Philippines. I was very much looking forward to visiting Manila. None of my reading, however, prepared me for the wife of the Philippine President, Imelda Marcos, AKA "The Dragon Lady." Our ambassador and his wife warned me about Mrs. Marcos, a striking former beauty queen with flamboyant tastes and a strong personality. We met at the ambassador's residence to discuss a schedule of site visits for Mrs. Nixon while Mr. Nixon was engrossed in presidential activities. They told me that I could plan away, anything I wished, but that ultimately Imelda would be in charge and would do as she pleased. They also advised me that Imelda's current project was a new cultural center and that she was pressuring the United States to purchase the giant crystal chandeliers she had selected for the interior. The Ambassador told me that the subject would undoubtedly come up, and I should forewarn Mrs. Nixon.

Modern first ladies are expected to have projects or special interests of some sort. Mrs. Kennedy redecorated the White House and Lady Bird Johnson promoted beautification of America's highways and public spaces. Hillary Clinton advised the country, shortly after arriving at the White House, that she was uninterested in lady's tea parties and promptly inserted herself into the policy arena by plumping for a national health care system. Mrs. Nixon was far from being the "Plastic Pat" portrayed by the some of the press. She knew that the public had elected her husband and not her. She tried to assist him by being a good political wife. In this, she was very successful and became the "most admired woman in America" in the opinion polls.

Mrs. Nixon was very down to earth. She had raised her younger brothers after their parents died when she was just a teenager. During the Depression, people helped each other in times of need. Volunteerism became an important element in her life. As first lady, she wanted to use her prominence to promote successful volunteer efforts and to amplify the accomplishments of volunteers. She believed that this was a more effective way to solve small scale local needs than any government program. As I was the person responsible for her schedule on the Asian trip, she told me to find examples of people helping each other. She wanted her visit to encourage such work and draw attention to volunteerism American style.

In the United States volunteers are a part of the culture and everything from hospitals to disaster relief depend upon corps of willing volunteers to augment the paid staff and multiply their efforts. This is not necessarily true in other countries, where there is often a sense that such things are the responsibility of the extended family, or the government. When I asked the embassy staff in Manila if they knew of any such examples, they couldn't come up with anything. Finally, someone gave me a name to call at Catholic Charities. Sure enough, they knew of a place that sounded like just what I was looking for.

In one of the poorest sections of Manila stood a small, ramshackle building with the sign "Kansas" over the door. Buildings age quickly in the tropics, but Kansas looked as though it had stood there a hundred years. It was a graphic example of good people living in bad neighborhoods. The local citizenry had organized the neighborhood center Kansas. If someone needed a person to look out for her children, or to watch over his elderly parent, or to provide rice for dinner, Kansas would provide such assistance. This was a real discovery. I could hardly wait to bring our First Lady to publicize its efforts. My team mapped out a schedule and counted this stop as a potential highlight.

That evening the embassy arranged a dinner for the advance team. I found myself sitting next to the Commander of the Navy's huge facility at Subic Bay. He regaled me with stories about things disappearing on the base. His tales gave me the impression that a general presumption prevailed on the part of the entire Philippine population: if you were not actually holding, using or driving something, you were assumed to have abandoned it and were no longer concerned about ownership. The locals had appropriated the base fire truck by the simple expedient of driving it through the front the gate with the lights flashing and the siren wailing. They had managed to cart off a half mile of anchor chain without leaving trace of how it had been accomplished. He concluded by telling me that he "figured that everything on the base had already been stolen. They just hadn't come by for it yet."

I returned to Manila several weeks later with the presidential party to find that Mrs. Marcos had modified my schedule. She refused to allow Mrs. Nixon to go to Kansas. Our embassy officials told me that they had gotten word that she would "burn it down" if we went there. Instead, we went to an idyllic orphanage outside of town with beautiful buildings and well-scrubbed kids holding flowers for Mrs. Nixon. At the entrance stood a large, freshly painted sign proclaiming that we were entering the *Nayon ng Kabataan Orphanage*, "*A project of the First Lady of the Philippines, Mrs. Imelda Romulaldez Marcos.*"

It got worse. I was riding in the follow-up security car on the way back to Manila from the orphanage when the agent who was driving announced that the route had just been changed. When he radioed the lead car in the motorcade to ask the reason, we were informed that Mrs. Marcos wanted to show Mrs. Nixon the new cultural center. And when we arrived, Mrs. Marcos prodded Mrs. Nixon about the US government making a gift of chandeliers. Mrs. Nixon, having been through the drill before, told Mrs. Marcos that the Department of State and the Congress had to approve such a donation, not she.

Perhaps it was because she sensed my restrained indignation, but that night when I returned to my hotel from the state dinner at Malacanang, the Philippine White House, there was a beautiful pair of snakeskin shoes for my wife with a card signed by Imelda Marcos. They didn't fit Connie, so we gave them away — an act that I regretted some years later, when the story of the Marcos' financial pillage of their country came out. It seems Mrs. Marcos had a closet with over 1,000 pairs of shoes and she often gave them away after only wearing them once.

I hadn't done any better with my Dragon Lady than Terry had with his.

23. A Boat Ride in Bangkok

In the middle of the Asian trip, the President planned to spend some extra time in Bangkok, Thailand as a rest and relaxation stop, to recuperate a bit from the jetlag and exhaustion that accompany such whirlwind tours. The President also took the opportunity to sneak into Vietnam and spend the afternoon with our combat troops. I certainly welcomed the chance to rest; I was whipped. I had been under a great deal of pressure and traveling constantly for almost 20 days.

Having some time off from her schedule of official duties, Mrs. Nixon wanted to do some touring and see the city's attractions. She had admired the *klong* boats when she visited Bangkok in 1952 as the vice president's wife, but had not had any opportunity to ride in one. Now, she wanted to see them through the eyes of an ordinary visitor. Before the advance trip she was quite specific in her instructions to me: a klong boat, with a klong boat pilot, so she could enjoy a typical tourist experience. She did not want the Thais to turn the tour into a "big deal" and do anything special for her.

Prior to the advance, I had never been to Bangkok and I had no idea about what she was requesting, but I assured her that I would arrange a klong boat trip. After all, how difficult could it be?

The klongs are a series of canals that transect the city and serve as major arteries of commerce; traffic on the streets was very congested. The klongs are lined with buildings on stilts, ranging from quite grand houses to bamboo shacks. There was no evidence of zoning or urban planning; people lived next to commercial buildings, also on stilts. There was even some industrial activity, such as boat building. People lived their whole lives on the klongs, dumped raw sewage into the klongs, washed their clothes in the klongs, and brushed their teeth in the klongs. The water of the klongs is a gray brown color that is hard to describe, and they have a foul odor. You could sense that any accidental dip in the water would disintegrate all the elastic in your underwear.

However, life along the klongs was colorful. There were fruit and vegetable dealers hustling their wares from dugout canoes, very unstable craft. It seemed miraculous that they never upset, but as the penalty for tipping over was a dunking in the klong, the incentive to keep their balance was high. Most of the boats were paddle propelled, but every minute or so a long, narrow craft, maybe twenty feet long and three feet wide, would come zooming along at high speed with his wake causing sheer terror in the paddlers. These klong boats were powered by motors unlike anything Mercury ever contemplated; the motor was attached in line with a 10- or 12-foot propeller shaft. Apparently, the klongs were not deep enough for conventional outboards and some smart Thai had come up with an innovation. And that's what Mrs. Nixon wanted to ride in: a typical klong boat.

When I discussed the First Lady's desires with the Thai officials, they couldn't understand why she wanted to visit the filthy klongs at all. Why not another tea party with the Queen, or a second tour through the Temple of the Emerald Buddha, or luncheon with the wife of the minister in charge of banana production? The klongs? Was I sure?

Yes, I was sure; and when I had them convinced, I outlined our needs. A *clean* klong boat for Mrs. Nixon, a Secret Service agent, a guide and myself, three klong boats for the press corps and an additional klong boat for the Secret Service. They bowed and smiled and nodded.

Then the Thais started over. They politely suggested I might like to use one of their naval craft. Perhaps the Admiral's barge? No, I said. I wanted a typical klong boat, with a typical klong driver and I wanted to go down a typical klong. Ahh, exclaimed the Thais, *typical*. They bowed and smiled and nodded again. The Thais are a very polite people.

I brought Mrs. Nixon to the appointed location at the appointed hour. The Thais escorted us onto a mahogany cruiser with a Thai navy crew and a snappy commodore in command. There was a kind of houseboat for the press. The Secret Service high-speed security boat promptly got stuck in the mud. Worse, the Thais had gathered up every school child in six counties and stationed them, shoulder to shoulder, along the klong in their blue and white school uniforms, with little paper American flags and a forced enthusiasm.

Mrs. Nixon was disappointed. The press was irritated. I was tense as hell. The Secret Service abandoned ship and got another security boat. But it was hard to be angry. The Thais were bowing, smiling and nodding.

This, I decided, really was typical.

24. THE BUCHAREST BLONDE

Air Force Two dove through the cloud cover over the Carpathian Mountains, a "stone curtain" that separates most of Romania from the rest of Europe. This little-known country was the one we had been most looking forward to visiting and we were all excited.

When I heard about the assignment to plan a trip to Romania, I had asked my friend Dick Allen to join me for lunch in the Navy Mess. Allen had been Nixon's foreign policy advisor during the 1968 campaign and was now Henry Kissinger's deputy on the National Security Council. (Allen later became the head of the NSC under President Reagan.) Dick was an expert on the Soviet bloc and I wanted to get his thoughts on the trip. Would the Romanians try any funny business?

Allen told me that he rather thought the Romanians would try to avoid any potential embarrassments, as this trip was far too important to Ceausescu's prestige. However, he would not be surprised if the Soviet espionage department tried to "slip the meat out of our sandwich" in some way, in order to embarrass the Romanians. I asked what they might do and he said, "Oh, you know, girls and that sort of thing." He advised me to stay alert. I thanked Dick and we agreed to meet after the trip for a debriefing. He would turn out to be remarkably prescient

We landed in Bucharest just as night fell, and we were not able to view much of the city on the way in from the airport. We went directly to the Ambassador's residence for a reception and briefing. I don't recall much that was said, except that we were told it was safe to wander around the city on our own. The visit of the president of the United States was a very big event for the Romanians. They were pulling out all the stops to impress us and ensure that we had a memorable time.

After the meeting we were taken to the hotel Athénée Palace. The baggage crew had delivered the baggage and were guarding it in the lobby. We were reminded, again, that the embassy had a control room in the hotel that would be manned 24 hours a day. All confidential material in our luggage and briefcases should be stored there when not in our immediate possession.

I retrieved my B4 bag and headed upstairs to my room, after agreeing to meet in the bar later with Robert Taylor and William Hawthorn. Taylor, a wonderful gentleman, was the special agent in charge of the White House Secret Service detail. He had been on Nixon's detail when he was vice president. He had also been with Nixon when they were caught in a street riot in Caracas, Venezuela and had risked his life getting Nixon out of it.

Bill Hawthorne was a young agent on the First Lady's detail who had been assigned to work the Bucharest stop as the special agent in charge. It was an honor for Hawthorne to be selected as the agent responsible for Bucharest, but he was just the man for the job. He had a graduate degree in public affairs and went on to become an assistant to the secretary of the Treasury. Bill Hawthorne and I were destined to work together many times and became close friends.

The Athénée Palace, now a Hilton, was a pre-war hotel that was architecturally charming in an old world, kind of worn down at the heels sort of way. When I got to my room, I immediately observed a floor-to-ceiling mirrored box constructed against the middle of one wall. It projected into the room about twelve inches and was three feet wide and just the right size, to my fertile imagination, to conceal a camera in the guise of a ventilation duct. As I sleep in my skivvies, I immediately set about covering the mirror with the bed cover and the cord from the window blinds. When finished, I felt reasonably secure from prying eyes. I then left to join my friends at the bar for a nightcap.

The lounge was jumping. At 10:00 PM on a Sunday night there was a band playing American music, a crowded dance floor, and several hundred customers imbibing and having a good time. Coming from a society where Sunday was traditionally a quiet evening for recuperation from the rigors of Saturday night, we were amazed. The Commies were enjoying the good life.

We stood about rather awkwardly, not knowing what to do, when we were approached by a very attractive blonde lady who introduced herself as the hotel interpreter and asked if she could be of service. We hemmed and hawed about wishing for a table. The next thing we knew, she went up to a table on the edge of the dance floor, said something to the two couples that caused them to rise promptly, take their drinks and vacate. She then waved us over and, sitting down with us, ordered up a round of drinks. We ordered beers. She took an American bourbon, pronouncing it booor-Bahn, in a delightful accent. She said it was the first booor-Bahn she had ever had, but she downed it as though she had been weaned on the stuff. In fact, her generation was weaned on movies that featured American bourbon and history lessons that featured the Bourbons of French royalty, and the two blended together in the popular imagination to create an extra aura of elegance for Kentucky whisky.

We were certainly impressed with the effort the Romanians were making to be friendly and hospitable. We were also impressed by the clientele in the lounge. They were pretty well dressed and seemed prosperous. Then, after a pleasant and interesting hour with our new friend, we asked for the check, but she said the hotel would pick up the tab. Maybe Communism was working in Romania!

I had just undressed and was about to climb into bed when I heard a knock at my door. I wrapped a towel around my waist and opened up to find the blonde lady, who pushed her way in and made a grab for my towel. I had two instant memories. The first was Richard Allen's warning and the second was an admonition from my wife: "Don't drink the water and stay away from the local women. Both carry strange diseases." I told the blonde that I was married, and tired; and I pushed her out the room before she made another pull at my towel. I immediately called Hawthorne and told him to expect a visitor. She knocked at his door while we were on the phone. As I turned out the light, I sadly ruminated about what James Bond would have done.

I was leaving the next day to go on to London but Bill Hawthorn was to remain in Bucharest, preparing for the President's arrival in two weeks. Would he see any more of the "blonde lady"?

White House Secret Service agents seemed to be cut from the same bolt of cloth. While on duty, they were all dead serious. Off duty, they were likeable, outgoing, fun loving, gregarious people. It was therefore quite natural that friendships would develop between members of the *Securitate*, the Romanian security force, and US agents. People were invited home for dinner. Bill Hawthorne even spent the weekend at a private resort on the Black Sea with the Romanian colonel who was responsible for all security relating to the visit.

As Hawthorne related it to me, that weekend he and the Colonel were sitting around, drinks in hand. Bill suggested that he had a question for the Colonel that was really none of his business, but he would like to ask it anyway. The Colonel said, "Ask away," or the equivalent; and Bill observed that everywhere he went a particular blonde woman kept cropping up. Why did the Colonel, who, after all, was supplying Hawthorne with a car and driver, feel it necessary to keep additional tabs on him? But the Colonel said, "What blonde lady? She's not one of ours." And he promised to look into it.

As best we could tell, the mysterious seductress was a Soviet agent after all. Whoever she was, the Colonel put an end to her activities. Of course, this meant an abrupt end to the James Bond fantasy and I never got to see her again, much less the chance to push her out of my bed. The use of attractive women to lure the opposition is known, in espionage circles, as a "honey trap." Putting such professionals up against a few tired men far from home hardly seems fair.

When Nixon arrived and departed, tens of thousands of cheering people lined the long straight road from the airport to the city. Crowd building is certainly easy in a tightly organized country. The road was lined with trees, behind each of which lurked a man in a baggy suit. To this surfeit of security was added a soldier with a Kalashnikov at "present arms" every 15 or 20 feet along both sides of the road. The road had been cleaned, the curbs freshly painted, buildings repaired and vegetation trimmed. The Romanians were doing their best to impress us. I could not but think of imperial Russia's Minister Potemkin and Empress Catherine. Still, it was effective. We left with a much different view of an Eastern bloc country than we had expected. Maybe there was something to detente after all.

When I got back to Washington, I was pleased to be able to assure Dick Allen that he was such a student of the Soviets that he could predict their activities. But, I shall always wonder about the beautiful blonde in my bedroom.

Is it possible she was just freelancing?

25. Staff Director to the First Lady

Bob Haldeman was a perfectionist. He was also highly organized, very detail oriented, and equipped with Mensa Society brainpower; not much escaped his notice. He was, in short, a formidable figure as the chief of staff. And he was unhappy.

The reason for Bob's current angst was the President's displeasure with the quality of work coming out of the East Wing of the White House, where the First Lady's staff conducted business. Herb Klein, the President's director of communications, had recommended Gerry van der Heuvel to be Mrs. Nixon's press secretary because she was a recent past president of the Women's National Press Club. But, Herb was not familiar with her skills. As it turned out, if Hubert Humphrey had won the election, Gerry van der Heuvel probably would have been his wife Muriel's press secretary, as she was a nominal democrat. Gerry had been a working reporter, and a pretty good one, but her strong suit was not management and organization. She and Lucy Winchester, the social secretary, were at the same management level. Neither had authority over the other. Unfortunately, they were also at the same skill level with regard to organization.

Lucy was the daughter of a wealthy contributor from Kentucky. She brought with her some finely tuned social skills, but that was not what the job essentially required. The President did not like socializing but, if he had to have parties, he wanted to maximize their political benefit. He wanted the First Lady's staff to plan events and be proactive in making the most of the occasion in a political sense. They were not there to consult with the White House florist's office regarding the coordination of colors.

In addition to the President's and Haldeman's concerns, the good ladies of the press were in a state of high dudgeon. They too were aggrieved about the management failures and disorganization in the First Lady's press office. Furthermore, as protective feminists, there was a growing resentment of the men of the West Wing meddling in affairs traditionally within the East Wing's purview. The Asian trip and my role, as it seemed to the press, as Mrs. Nixon's staff director, was the last straw. Something had to be done. Yet, in July, I began to be pulled in deeper.

THE WHITE HOUSE

WASHINGTON

Aboard Air Force One

MEMORANDUM

July 23, 1969

FOR: MR. CHARLES STUART

The President's News Summary reported that Frans Koltun of the PHILADELPHIA INQUIRER (7/13) writes that Mrs. Nixon came through her West Coast trip with flying colors as she showed her ability to travel with grace and stamina. She never lost her cool and proved herself a warm, hard-working, winning human being. The trip also demonstrated how blessed the US is with so many hard-working volunteers. Julie is an enchanting, natural girl with a radiant and quick smile. "She's a winner."

The President wants to be sure that letters are always prepared for Mrs. Nixon, Julie and Tricia, thanking reporters for favorable stories like this, just as is the President's practice.

He wants you to talk this over with Mrs. Nixon.

H. R. Haldeman

The President continued to direct Bob to get me involved. Two weeks later I received the following action memo from Haldeman:

THE WHITE HOUSE

WASHINGTON

MEMORANDUM

September 9, 1969

FOR: MR. CHARLES STUART

Following up on the First Lady question, as I told you the other day, the President wants you to be the West Wing man who maintains the current watch over and interest in East Wing operations and the First Lady's schedule, etc. This does not mean that you step into an operating role over there, but rather that you function as his representative from this side in whatever way you can be helpful over there.

As one case in point, he wants to be sure that a competent advance man from our group is assigned to all public appearances of Mrs. Nixon, Tricia and Julie. This would be your responsibility. He also wants you to ride herd on Keogh and his group and be sure that the same kind of suggested remarks are prepared for Mrs. Nixon and the girls as are prepared for the President. He considers this, in fact, to be more important than the material prepared for him, since he is able to handle his on his own, if necessary, where they are not.

I have raised this several times with Keogh and his people, but the results have not been totally satisfactory, I guess; so it's going to require some continuing follow up on your part.

I would appreciate a *very brief* memo from you at the end of each week on how this is going and what, if any, problems we have that need attention.

H.R. HALDEMAN

Two weeks later this was followed up with another memorandum regarding Tricia Nixon, the eldest daughter of the President. Tricia had the reputation of being somewhat difficult to work with. However, when I had organized a trip for her to Norfolk, VA to be Queen of the Azalea Festival, we had gotten along just fine. I presumed this assignment was a result of that experience.

THE WHITE HOUSE

WASHINGTON

MEMORANDUM

FOR: MR. CHARLES STUART

Last week Tricia Nixon made a trip to Philadelphia to attend the opening of an exhibit at the museum there, and it was very successful. She got a front-page story in the Philadelphia paper, a good national wire service story and some good television coverage.

Because of the success of this visit, the President is most anxious that she do more things of this sort, and Tricia has agreed to do this kind of thing on about a once-a-week basis.

The President would like you to take the responsibility of making sure that all opportunities of this kind are carefully explored, and that we take the initiative in developing such opportunities.

I would suggest that you first get a full run down on the Philadelphia thing itself and how it was handled and what can be done, and then you might talk to Tricia about her views on the kinds of things she can do most effectively.

You should then consult with Chapin about schedule opportunities that may exist as a result of things that the President is invited to do that Tricia could pinch hit for him on. The same is also true of invitations to the First Lady. Then we could also look for opportunities on our own.

The point here is to get Tricia out into areas other than Washington and New York. She obviously will get much more attention in smaller cities and in places removed from Washington. We should, of course, keep in mind the political desirability of visits to Virginia and New Jersey at the present time, and to such places as Minnesota, Texas, etc. in the future.

The President feels, too, that Tricia would be especially effective in the Mid-West and the South and that we should definitely look for opportunities there. Please give me a report on what you are doing on this in a week or two.

H.R. Haldeman

I had to tell Bob that what the President and he had instructed me to do was not the right solution (imagine, telling the president of the United States that he had a bad idea!) particularly in light of the concern of the distaff press corps. The last thing they wanted to see was me in the middle, between the East and West Wings as a "coordinator." What was really needed was a complete reorganization of the first lady's office so that her people didn't require someone from the president's staff to monitor and supervise their work. This group should also be in charge of the girls' scheduling and various types of "family" news. The Johnson girls had apparently not been politically active and had shunned the press. Tricia and Julie were young adults, attractive, and active in the White House. The press corps was always eager for news about the Nixon girls.

I proposed to undertake a staff analysis and recommend changes. I would also develop some guidelines for a political/public relations program for the First Lady as well as set forth how it should be implemented. In addition, I suggested that the East Wing have a female staff member who was an experienced advance person. I told Bob that I would train whoever was selected. After some discussion with the President, Bob agreed with my suggestion.

I spent more than a week on the assignment, interviewed numerous people and researched how previous East Wing staffs had been organized. I produced a 57-page report, tabbed and footnoted in the best West Wing style. The President and Bob were in San Clemente when I finished my work, so I presumed I would wait until they returned and meet with them to discuss my proposals. This was not to be the case. Bob instructed me to catch the next military courier flight that shuttled between El Toro Marine Air Station in California and Andrews Air Force Base, in Washington. He was apparently still catching heat from Nixon and wanted to give him something to read.

I made a large number of suggestions but, most importantly, I recommended that Gerry van den Heuvel and several other senior staff members be replaced. I proposed that the position of *Staff Director to the First Lady* be created. This person would also serve as the press secretary. The staff director should have managerial experience in a public relations field, and should be an accomplished writer and a creative innovator as well as a loyal Republican. The social secretary would become a subservient position. The ship needed one competent captain, not two poor first mates.

I went to San Clemente and made my presentation during a lunch (not my favorite timing). At 6'4," 200 pounds, I was a champion eater. My mother had taught me not to talk with my mouth full, so I did not like to have my meal interrupted by having to speak, especially to Haldeman, who sat and enjoyed his lunch and asked me a lot of questions.

When I finished going over my proposal he asked some more questions, and finished with, "I'll get back to you." Bob could never be accused of exhibiting human emotion in his role of chief of staff. He was all business. When he called you on the telephone, there was no small talk. He just began speaking about the issue at hand. True to fashion, there were no "good job, Chuck's" or even an "atta-boy." Nothing. I hung around San Clemente for a day, enjoying the Pacific sun, and returned to the White House.

When Nixon got back from San Clemente, Connie got a got a call at her office at C & P Telephone Company from Larry Higby, Bob Haldeman's administrative assistant. "Could you come in to meet with Bob on Thursday afternoon at 2:00 PM?" Connie said "yes," and then called me to ask what Bob wanted. I didn't know and couldn't even guess. Never in my wildest imagination did I anticipate him asking Connie to take over as Pat Nixon's staff director and implement the suggestions in my study.

Connie had met Mrs. Nixon and had even helped her hold a press conference in Boston during the campaign. Then a film producer for AT&T, Connie had been shooting a movie on Cape Cod at the same time I was in Boston. She had come down for several days to help out. That was also when she first met Bob Haldeman. After I went to work for Nixon, she had seen Bob in the White House on several occasions. Apparently Bob had suggested to both the President and Mrs. Nixon that Connie be engaged as Staff Director and Press Secretary. They agreed it was a good idea.

Connie quietly started work, possibly the only secret successfully kept from press in the Nixon White House. The announcement of her appointment was made a week later, in mid-October 1969, at a press conference in the White House theater. It was attended by some 50 or 60 members of the press corps who had been invited, ostensibly, to hear Mrs. Nixon speak. She introduced Connie and graciously left the stage. Ron Ziegler, the President's press secretary, and I watched in privacy from the projection booth. After some fifteen minutes, Ziegler turned to me and said, "She'll do fine."

Connie held the position for three years. She held two press briefings a week, the first such scheduled briefings ever for a first lady, on the activities of Mrs. Nixon and the Nixon family. No doubt the press corps believes to this day that I got my wife installed in the position, but I did not. She earned it herself.

No doubt, too, Bob Haldeman felt that he could control Connie through me. If he had only asked, I could have disabused him of that notion. Connie and Bob conducted a lively exchange of interoffice memoranda during her term in office. Her staff came to call his directives "H grams." An example of one such interchange follows:

THE WHITE HOUSE

WASHINGTON

MEMORANDUM

November 5, 1971

FOR: CONNIE STUART

SUBJECT: Thursday Evening Entertainment

As is obvious in reading this morning's stories on last night's entertainment, there is a serious problem procedurally in the way we are handling these things. I would like to know who was responsible for selecting the entertainment, who checked out the backgrounds of the entertainers, how this incident happened, and what we are doing to make sure similar incidents don't occur in the future.

H.R. HALDEMAN

HRH:LH:pm

Apparently, the Washington Post had published an article by Sally Quinn about a longhaired member of the band. Connie's reply follows:

THE WHITE HOUSE

WASHINGTON

MEMORANDUM   November 15, 1971

TO: H. R. HALDEMAN

FROM: CONSTANCE STUART

In response to your memo concerning entertainment at the Gandhi State Dinner.

As you know, Mrs. Nixon selects the entertainers for White House functions based on many suggestions from the President's staff, State Department and our own resource files. Mrs. Nixon is consulted on all facets of entertainment as it develops.

The background of the entertainers is checked out by Secret Service, FBI, Len Garment's shop, contacts in the entertainment business like Taft Schreiber, etc. Unknown accompanists who are brought along by major performers are very hard for anybody to check out. We check them out through the guest artist as best we can.

I do not know how Sally Quinn followed our hairy and bearded friend around and got her story. I'm sure you know you that Sally Quinn is one of the most vicious social writers on the *Post* and that she chews up everybody, not just us. The story she wrote on the state dinner was very nice and one of the straightest we've ever had.

As I stick my head slowly into the noose, may I say that I found Sally's story about the hairy guitarist quite funny and no reflection on the White House whatsoever. I'm sure you aren't indicating that we shouldn't have longhairs in the White House just because they don't shave.

And if you ever find a way to insure that Beverly Sill's zipper won't pop, Anna Moffo's neckline won't plunge, Johnny Cash doesn't loose his baby in the Lincoln bedroom and accompanists don't turn out to be more difficult to deal with than the artist, we would appreciate your counsel. We do the very best we can, but the unknown looms menacingly when dealing with the entertainment profession. It's kind of like dealing with politicians.

I understand that the President did like Villella and wanted an encore. That's what counts.

Connie is a perfectionist. She is also smart, highly organized, and very detail oriented; not much escapes her notice. She was, in short, a formidable figure as the staff director to the first lady. Most importantly, as an attractive woman, with red hair and a temperament to match, she had an unfair advantage over Bob Haldeman. Poor Bob never had a chance.

In time, Connie became known as "the Haldeman of the East Wing." It was a sobriquet with which she was pleased and it suited her.

26. STARLIGHT TOUR

Due to the Vietnam War, much of the youth of America turned against the national leadership. They rioted and protested to the degree that, in his final year in office, President Johnson was virtually a prisoner in the White House. When the TV humorists suggested that Johnson was only safe speaking on aircraft carriers and at military academies, they were not far from the truth. During the 1968 campaign, Nixon, too, was picketed, but not to the same extent as Hubert Humphrey. Often, we advance men were able to make the point to the protesters that Nixon wanted to end the war and had played no part in its origin. However, after he'd been in office a few months, the nation's youth began to turn on him, too. It became apparent that we needed to reach out to this segment of the population that had been so destructive to the political fortunes of Lyndon Johnson.

In the spring of 1969, John Ehrlichman directed me to set up a meeting with a small group of dissident youth from around the country. Someone suggested that this be done at Airlie House, a private convention center in the Virginia countryside. Airlie was about an hour's drive from Washington, where we would be safe from prying reporters. I took an army helicopter out to inspect the facility and make the arrangements. It seemed ideal for our purposes. John Ehrlichman gave me a list of invitees who were somewhere between the Weathermen (a particularly violent protest movement of the time) and plain vanilla student anti-war leaders. These included:

Joseph Rhodes — President of the Student Body, California Institute of Technology

Xandra Kaden — Chairman, Students for a Reconstructed University (Columbia)

David Thomas — President of the Student Body, University of Missouri

Bob Henderson — President of the Black Student Union, University of Massachusetts

Charley Palmer — President of the Student Body at UC Berkeley

Wade Norris — President of Student Body, Duke University

David Mixner — Senator McCarthy's young campaign manager

Arrangements were made to bring them to Airlie for the day. John and I and several others met with them and discussed their views. I doubt that either side much influenced the other but it was the first step of an outreach program. Although they had been driven to Airlie by White House motor pool cars, the meeting ran long and we ordered up choppers for the return trip as we had offered to give them a tour of the West Wing. We could do this without the approval of the Secret Service because Nixon was away and there was no chance of running into him. I remember thinking how ironic it was that these anti-war kids were now in the same UH-1 "slicks" that, half way around the world, were ferrying other kids their own age into combat.

Building bridges to America's youth remained a goal of the administration during the entire first term. There were a number of proposals put forth regarding how this might be accomplished. All, however, involved the person of the President and were deemed too risky.

President Richard Nixon was the most politically astute and attuned man in the White House. His skills had been honed in seven political campaigns, four of them for national office. He could just sense things that needed to be done, groups of the electorate whom we needed to court, areas of the country that needed attention, and how to accomplish the objective.

He thought that while he might be unable to visit college campuses, his wife might just be able to slip in and meet with students and not get picketed in the process. I was asked to organize such a trip as I had earlier organized a trip for Mrs. Nixon to encourage volunteerism. I was told to visit five states: Michigan, Kentucky, Ohio, Colorado and Missouri. Beyond that, I was on my own. I was in total control, a phenomenon that never occurs with presidential trips that always involve layer upon layer of participants in the planning and approval process. I put together a trip that included visits to Michigan State University, the University of Kentucky, the University of Cincinnati, the University of Colorado and the School of the Ozarks. The trip was ostensibly to visit student volunteer projects but it was really to attempt to bond the Administration with the youth of America.

I will not relate all of the effort that went into the enterprise except that it took a number of weeks of fieldwork to put together a four-day tour by Mrs. Nixon. It also required a significant amount of technical support by other agencies of the government. The Secret Service told me that it was the biggest trip ever undertaken by a first lady traveling without her husband. It involved nearly a dozen events and included meetings with students in each state. One of the emblematic events was the visit to the University of Colorado at Boulder.

Most of the meetings were with "safe" students groups who were not likely to demonstrate or picket or create unpleasant scenes that would generate unfavorable publicity. Obviously, no Eastern liberal schools, where the anti-war movement was the strongest, were included. The exception was the University of Colorado, hardly a placid institution at the time.

Colorado was a hotbed of radicalism. The Students for a Democratic Society (SDS) were highly organized as were a number of other ad hoc groups. The Denver area had experienced some 28 unsolved bombings of banks, corporate offices and power lines. A National Guard armory had been burglarized and weapons stolen. It was considered a dangerous place and the Secret Service was apprehensive. Still, I believed that we needed a visit to such a location in order for our efforts to have credibility.

When the First Lady landed at the Denver airport, the Secret Service received a death threat. A *Women's Wear Daily* reporter overheard a discussion about it on the Secret Service radio net and in a grotesquely thoughtless maneuver sprang it on Mrs. Nixon, asking what she thought about "the threat." Maintaining her poise, Pat said that she "didn't know anything about it." Part of our job was to prevent such upsetting scenes, and making sure any gaffe that does occur will not be repeated. We took the opportunity to educate this reporter on the etiquette of protecting national figures psychologically as well as physically, and enabling them to go on with their jobs.

I met with the President of the University of Colorado and discussed with him our desire to meet with a small group of his students. I told him that I understood that he and his fellow administrators could not guarantee against untoward events; indeed, they had no control over the campus themselves when it came to anti-war demonstrations. I asked him to organize a meeting with a dozen of the radical student leaders for me alone, without any faculty. I wanted to see if I could reason with them. While he was pleased that his university had been selected for a visit by the First Lady and accompanying press, he was reluctant to go through with it. The specter of possibly finding himself hosting a major student riot, on national television, was daunting.

I met with the students, longhaired, bearded young men and unkempt girls, much different from the well-groomed, tweedy appearance of the college students of a dozen years earlier. I told them that I wanted to bring the First Lady of the United States to meet with them. I wanted their guarantee of secrecy until after the meeting. I also wanted their personal assurances that they would not organize any demonstrations or picketing of any kind. If they couldn't give me these assurances, we would not come. They were all, of course, anti-establishment. I was quite possibly the first conservative Republican with whom they had ever had a serious conversation. At first, there was antagonism, which softened to neutrality, which evolved, after several hours of conversation, into acceptance. They agreed. I felt I had won them over and I decided to risk setting up a meeting with Mrs. Nixon.

One young man in particular, the President of the Student Government, held radical views but seemed to be a responsible leader. I was to meet with him several times in the weeks to come. I even visited with him in his apartment, where I saw a marijuana plant for the first time, potted and growing in the living room. A wedding gift, I was told.

Mrs. Nixon did not possess the political skills of her husband. She did not relish public speaking. However, she was a smart woman. She had been listening to political speeches for nearly 25 years and she knew what to say and how to say it. She also knew how to dodge a question she didn't want to answer. In her meeting with the students in Colorado, she was confronted with an audience filled with gritty-looking people wearing "peace" buttons — the students had honored their pledge to me not to demonstrate; I wasn't smart enough to include buttons in the definition of "demonstration." She didn't flinch. When several questioners asked her about the war, she deftly reminded them that the purpose of the visit was to draw attention to the good things that student volunteers were accomplishing.

The trip was a great success. Connie had signed up some 40 members of the press including AP, UPI, *US News and World Report*, *Time* and *Newsweek* magazines, the *Washington Post*, all of the TV networks as well as the major women's magazines and foreign press, to cover the trip. When the crews from the local markets were included, there were as many as 75 members of the press.

Mrs. Nixon was a real star. This was the first time she had been out on her own, away from her husband on a major media trip. She was well received everywhere she went. She easily conversed with the students. Most importantly, she got excellent news coverage — "good ink." This made the President happy. *Time* magazine said that Pat Nixon "filled her fourteen hour days with visits to the poor, the blind, the retarded, the aged and the outcast...." Commenting on the four stand-up press conferences, *The Washington Post* observed that a "facet of Mrs. Nixon's personality that reporters had not heretofore seen is her ability to face with poise and assurance a roomful of reporters and to express with ease and articulateness her interest in and concern for people." Such coverage made the President happy. "Starlight," her Secret Service code name, had proven to be most appropriate.

A word, here, about the female press corps that covered the East wing. I had considerable experience with them on the Asian trip, as well as the college trip, and had gotten to know several of the women quite well. Even though they were generally dealing with softer news, they worked at it as hard as if they were reporting on a news scoop of the first order. Indeed, the two wire service reporters, Helen Thomas (UPI) and Fran Lewin (AP), were more energetic than most of the other reporters, East or West wing. They were on deadline all the time and it showed. They had their own car in every motorcade, right behind the follow-up security car. I can still visualize them both, flinging open the car doors when the motorcade stopped, hitting the ground running, note pads in hand, skirts flying, hair akimbo, to Mrs. Nixon's car, in order not to miss anything that might be grist for their mill.

Helen Thomas went on to be the Dean of the Press Corps in the West Wing, the first female to be so honored. By tradition in the press corps, the wire service reporters rotate asking the first question at presidential press conferences and close with, "Thank you, Mr. President." Helen performed this duty with aplomb over the years. She never threw a "soft ball question," no matter who was President. Jacqueline Kennedy may have referred to the ladies of the press as "harpies"; I never saw them that way.

There was only one adverse incident in this entire program, and it was not caused by any student group. In Lansing, Michigan, at a volunteer center, several young people dressed as witches showered Mrs. Nixon with strips of paper on which was written, "If this were napalm, you'd be dead." The manager of the volunteer center was responsible for preventing this kind of assault, according to the terms of our agreement, but Mrs. Nixon took it in stride and even made light of it. The Secret Service, of course, thought differently.

I kept up a correspondence with the President of the Student Government at the University of Colorado and felt that I was making some headway into convincing him that the establishment wasn't all bad — that Republicans could be trusted. A year later, when he was in law school, he even asked me if I could get him a summer job with the Government. I called my friend, Richard Kleindienst, then the Deputy Attorney General, and he arranged an internship at the Department of Justice.

Several years later, Nixon resigned and Kleindienst was convicted of criminal conduct related to Watergate. I have often wondered what ever became of my young friend and whether my missionary work was in vain.

27. THE LAND OF THE RISING SUN

No sitting US president had ever visited Japan. Ulysses S. Grant went to Japan after he left the White House. Dwight Eisenhower was planning a trip when the US pilot Francis Gary Powers was shot down in his U2 airplane while spying on the Soviet Union, creating an embarrassing international incident. (For decades thereafter, the Red Army Museum in Moscow displayed wreckage from this aircraft. Tourists visiting during the cold war could thus enjoy the spectacle of Powers's downed plane while surrounded by Soviet soldiers.) The US government at first denied responsibility, but the international atmosphere turned sour and Eisenhower's advisors thought it prudent to cancel his trip to Japan due to student unrest. In these days of constant observation by satellites, the idea of spying in a country's sovereign air space no longer seems so shocking, but it was an outrage back then.

In 1970, the Japanese government, seeing that Nixon was traveling extensively but not in their direction, felt neglected. They alone among the major allies had never enjoyed a presidential visit, and they invited Nixon to Japan to open the World's Fair in Osaka. They did not know, nor did anyone else, of Nixon's plan regarding a visit to China.

Although such a notion was still in the dream stage, given the fact that China and Japan were historical enemies Nixon believed that his first trip to the Far East would have to be to China. However, with his highly tuned sensitivity for favorable public relations events, Nixon saw an opportunity. He told the Japanese that he was not yet ready to come to Japan; however, if they invited his daughter Julie and his son-in-law David Eisenhower, they would be willing to stand in for him. This put the Japanese in a diplomatic box. If the US President asked them to invite Julie and David Eisenhower to come for a visit, how could they refuse?

The Government of Japan invited David and Julie to the Fair, but not to the grand opening. That's diplomacy. And so it came to pass that Nixon and Haldeman sent for me on the afternoon of March 19, 1970 to come to the Oval Office.

When I arrived, Nixon was behind his desk. Bob was in his customary seat on the side. I was invited to sit down on the other side of the President's desk. Nixon explained that he wanted me to set up a trip to Japan for Julie and David. He also wanted them to go to Hong Kong, Taiwan, Korea and Alaska. He told me that I was to have full responsibility for the young people, what they did and where they went. He emphasized that I should not let the Department of State run the show, although I was certainly to use them for support.

I spent less than a half hour getting instructions on what would become the trip of a lifetime. Following is my *aide memoir*, dictated immediately after the meeting:

THE WHITE HOUSE

WASHINGTON

MEMORANDUM   March 19, 1970

FOR FILE:

FROM   Charles Stuart

RE: Meeting with President — David and Julie Trip

At 4:35 this afternoon the President met with H.R. Haldeman and me regarding the forthcoming trip of David and Julie Eisenhower to the Far East. We were joined from time to time by Dwight Chapin.

The President raised the following points:

He, the President, desires to pay all of David and Julie's expenses. It is his intention to give them each $3,000 (max tax free gift) which would be deposited in a special trip account. From this account I will purchase their airline tickets and will pay other bills incidental to travel and they will be able to draw on the account for purchases.

The President noted that the Eisenhowers should stay at the American Embassy in Japan, may wish to stay at the embassy in Korea, will probably be the guests of the Government in Taiwan and should stay at the Mandarin Hotel in Hong Kong.

The President emphasized that the purpose of this trip is for the young people to enjoy themselves, but they must also fulfill some ambassadorial-type obligations in each of the countries visited. The President does not want them to attend large dinners or receptions but felt that such events may be necessary in several countries. If Madame Chiang Kai-Shek desires to have a luncheon or dinner it should be accepted as should be a luncheon with the Crown Family in Japan and, since they are in Japan four or five days, perhaps an American Embassy reception. The President also noted that the American colony in Hong Kong had raised substantial monies for the Nixon Library and that a reception might be in order in that city.

The President was adamant that no gifts should be accepted from representatives of any country other than the head of state. He indicated that the Eisenhowers should deliver gifts to schools, welfare centers, etc. when such presentations would be appropriate. He specifically desires a substantial gift to be presented to the Nixon Library.

The President made passing remarks regarding the Ambassadors in each of the countries and drew special emphasis to the quality of our Ambassador in Taiwan.

The President suggested that David lay wreaths at appropriate memorials, but only to heroes of the host country and not to American soldiers.

The President believes that the Eisenhowers should visit schools and/or universities and felt that Hong Kong was an excellent place to visit a Chinese school and in Taiwan a university would be a safe stop.

The President stated that Linda Johnson's dress shop in Hong Kong was a reliable place for Julie to order clothes.

The President asks that we explore the possibility of visiting Alaska on the return from the Far East.

The President suggested that a briefing book be prepared by the State Department for immediate distribution to the Eisenhowers.

When at the World's Fair, it was the President's feeling that every exhibit should be visited in order not to slight any nation. He felt that a special emphasis should be placed on the American pavilion and that the Russian pavilion should also be thoroughly covered.

The President indicated a desire to use Pan American Airlines, if possible.

In conclusion, it became my feeling that the President was prepared to allow me substantial latitude in the scheduling and selecting processes. He was apparently pleased with the recent trip of Mrs. Nixon and implied that I should do as well for the Eisenhowers.

CC: H.R. Haldeman

Dwight Chapin

When I returned to my office, I called Bill Duncan, the Assistant Special Agent in Charge (ASAIC) of the White House detail. Bill was the agent responsible for the family's security. I told him we had an advance trip to make together. Duncan was another special friend in the Secret Service, a man admired by everyone as the "perfect agent," a role model for the younger men on the detail.

I then met with Julie and David Eisenhower, who told me that they did not have enough time to go to Taiwan, Hong Kong and Korea. Alaska was marginal. I should make arrangements for them to spend some time in a fishing camp, but nothing that could not be cancelled.

On the advance trip, Duncan and I flew commercial to Hawaii where the plane refueled and immediately left for Japan. We were on a Boeing 747, an aircraft that had recently been introduced and was having some teething problems. Nothing too serious; but they had a tendency to experience engine trouble in flight.

We left Honolulu and had just reached the "point of no return," that point in the flight when you are halfway to your destination, when the pilot announced that he had just shut down an engine; but, he said, there was nothing to worry about. The plane was fully capable of operating on three engines; it just wouldn't fly as fast. But shortly after that announcement came another. "Ladies and gentlemen, we have just lost another engine and I have elected to make an emergency landing on Wake Island. Please return to your seats and secure your seat belts."

The aircraft was filled with military personnel en-route to Vietnam via Japan, who, prior to the announcement, had been drinking, chatting up the stewardesses, wandering in the aisles and generally behaving as young bachelors do. After the announcement, the silence was deafening; several hundred macho young men shut down their activities.

We landed on Wake Island, a mile-long postage stamp in the Pacific. Wake was an island known only because of its capture by the Japanese during World War II. It was still garrisoned as an emergency stop for military aircraft. The Boeing 747 was too high for the rolling exit ramps so, after we came to a stop, we couldn't get off the aircraft. Further, Wake had no ground air conditioning equipment. We sat in the tropical sun and the temperature began to rise to near baking levels. Worse, the stewardesses quickly ran through their supply of cold beer, then the ice, soft drinks, and food. The final indignity was that the lavatories could not be emptied. They filled up and overflowed on the floor. We endured this for more than twelve hours before the necessary parts, flown in from Hawaii, could be installed and we took off. When the plane finally landed at Tokyo's Haneda airport, we had been on the plane over 19 hours.

Waiting for us at the airport with his car and driver was the deputy chief of mission, Richard Erickson, an outstanding Foreign Service officer. Erickson informed us that the Ambassador was waiting to meet with us and we were going directly to the embassy. As we walked through the airport with our luggage, we saw that several older Japanese men were dealing with the heat by sitting stripped to their underwear, pants and jackets neatly folded on the seats beside them. If only I could have done the same!

Ambassador Armin Meyer was a prototypical senior Foreign Service officer. Tall, handsome, intelligent, elegant, and cool and crisp in a natty blue suit. Duncan and I were crumpled, unshaven, bleary eyed, sweaty and odoriferous. I was embarrassed, but Meyer made us comfortable with his courtesy and an iced drink. He suggested that we go to our hotel and take a nap. He said we would reconvene later in the day. We were pleased to take his advice. When we met later, our pride was intact. Both Duncan and I "cleaned up well" and were prepared to represent the Nixon White House.

Meyer and Erickson had begun to receive requests from the Japanese Government for Julie and David to attend other events. This was common, whether in Oshkosh or Osaka — people feel that as long as the President (or his family) is so close, he should attend their son's cub scout meeting. Or the Chamber of Commerce fish fry. Or the regional semifinals of the national spelling bee. There were, of course, some "must do's." The Foreign Minister's luncheon, the dinner with the Osaka Prefecture, a meal with the Crown Prince and his sister, a press conference. We went over these and roughed out a schedule which consumed almost a week

One of the doctrines of advancing is that you must be intimately familiar with every place you are going to take the principal. Of course, with the president, this is an absolute. With Julie and David, Duncan and I felt we could relax the rules but we still had a week's worth of work and we enjoyed being American tourists in the Orient. We traveled around Japan with Dick Erickson who, with a long career spent in that country, proved to be an exceptional guide. Then it was back home to Washington to pick up Julie and David and depart again, this time on a US Government 707, the back-up aircraft to Air Force One. The Secret Service nixed the President's wishes to have them fly on Pam American.

There were seven of us on the trip; Nixon had sent his doctor, General Walter Tkach, and Duncan had enlisted two additional agents to serve as security guards. Tkach was a real gentleman of the old school. I once asked him which of his two prestigious titles, Doctor or General, he preferred I call him. He smiled and said, "Charles, just call me Walter!"

On the way over, Julie celebrated her 21st birthday. We had secretly brought on board a cake from the White House baker and held an impromptu party.

When we landed in Tokyo, we were welcomed by the Foreign Minister and his wife, Mr. and Mrs. Aichi. He was accompanied by our host and hostess for the week, Ambassador Togo, with his tall and attractive wife. These two exceptional people were personable, handsome, and better with our language than most Americans. As we were not accompanied by a gaggle of additional staff and hangers-on, Dr. Tkach and I became part of the "Suite of Honor." We were treated as principals, not as staff.

We had a wonderful week of luncheons, dinners, travel and entertainment with no untoward incidents. However, there were several events that remain highlighted in my memory.

At the luncheon hosted by the Foreign Minister we sat on the customary *tatami*, a straw mat placed directly on the floor, and ate from low tables. This was awkward for the men, but worse for the Western women as they had to contend with modesty issues caused by the mini skirts that were popular at the time. They managed!

Meals in the Orient generally involve many small portions of foods that are unidentifiable to the untrained eye and challenging for the unaccustomed palate. At this luncheon one of the courses involved the *ayu*. The ayu is a fish that lives in the interior rivers in Japan and is considered a delicacy. It is caught by the cormorant, a large and severely underprivileged bird in the Japanese scheme of things. The drama takes place at night when a small rowboat sets off from the shore with a charcoal fire in a metal embrasure at the bow. The fisherman paddles around until an ayu, attracted by the light, comes to the surface. Enter the cormorant, which has a string tied to his leg and a ring around his neck to prevent him from swallowing. The fisherman tosses the cormorant over the bow, where he catches the ayu. He tries to swallow the fish but cannot, due to the ring. The fisherman retrieves the poor bird with the string, removes the fish from his mouth, and tosses him over again. Thus the choice morsels are acquired for the best-laid tables.

And the ayu, still flopping, is popped in a skillet without any of the cleaning processes Westerners associate with the cooking of fish. Then, after a nominal period in the pot, the ayu is removed, put on a plate and served to unsuspecting visitors. He arrives, looking up at you, still filled with all of the organs that were necessary to his life including his stomach. The wife of an embassy officer, sitting next to me at the luncheon, cut into her ayu and found it full of half-digested baby shrimp, presumably a late night snack. She later told me that she could only hope that all of the other ayus were as elegantly stuffed with shrimp. Fortunately, the meal was accompanied by a large quantity of Kirin beer, with the help of which we were all able to maintain the necessary diplomatic graces.

We stayed in a guest house on the grounds of the Royal Palace, a leafy enclave in the very center of Tokyo. It was spared destruction during World War II. General McArthur recognized how important the Emperor was to the Japanese people and wanted to preserve their good will. The guest house was furnished in "Teutonic Boxy," a style which even the Salvation Army stopped accepting in the US some years ago. It was massive, dark and overstuffed. It certainly reflected the conservatism of the household keepers of the royal palace, the Geimusho. Unlike the White House, with a constantly changing political staff, the people around the Emperor did not come and go. They stayed and stayed. They became more and more powerful. Everything the Royal Family did had to be vetted by the Geimusho.

The bathroom was equipped with the normal Western-style fixtures, but dated. There was a cardboard sign that sat on the edge of the tub with the engaging notice: "Please keep the valve open for a while, because hot water is not splashing soon. Please try to contact room boy, in case you can't handle."

On the Fourth of July, it is customary for every US ambassador around the world to host a large party at his residence in recognition of that most American of holidays. We were back in Tokyo on July 4, and the Meyers held a fine celebration with the young Eisenhowers as the guests of honor.

The last night we were in Tokyo, Ambassador Togo asked me if he could host us to a simple dinner, just the Suite of Honor with the addition of Ambassador Meyer and his wife. I asked Julie and David, and of course, they agreed.

Tempura is, for my money, the Japanese cuisine most suited to Western palates. Togo had engaged an entire restaurant for the evening and we were ushered into a room of grand proportions with a square counter in the middle with 10 or 12 seats along each edge. The lighting was so dim that it was difficult to see. We were seated along the edge of the counter and faced into a dark void. After a dramatic pause, there was an audible click, a pump started and an elevator came up in the center of the void. As the elevator rose from some indeterminable depth, the lights also rose to reveal a kitchen with a white-suited chef standing at attention. When the elevator reached to full height, a foot above the floor level so that the chef was slightly higher than his seated patrons, it stopped. He bowed and placed a plate and chopsticks in front of each of us and then proceeded to dip shrimp and vegetables in a light batter and deep fry our tempura, whilst maintaining both a stony silence and countenance. At the end of a proscribed time period, by which time we had all had enough tempura, the chef produced a camera, bowed and raised a finger, seeking permission to take a picture. Julie nodded her assent, and the photo was snapped. The chef bowed again. A switch was thrown and the kitchen and chef disappeared as the lights went down and the elevator receded into the abyss. It was a stunning effect.

In their first diplomatic venture, David and Julie held a press conference for a large crowd of journalists and cameramen. David gave a speech at the Osaka Fair and offered toasts at the luncheons and dinners. They made no misstep, were gracious and pleasant, the very models of well-bred young marrieds.

Mr. and Mrs. Togo were famous in their country in a unique way. In the Russian-Japanese war of 1904, a Japanese admiral won a decisive victory in the battle of Taushima Bay. His name was Togo and he instantly became a major figure in modern Japanese history. He was the grandfather of the Ambassador's wife. Since there were no male heirs left in the lineage, the ambassador had cheerfully assumed his wife's family name. It was important that the Togo name be preserved, though not necessarily through a male heir. This custom is strange to European culture, but seems very sensible. I think the Japanese are onto something.

28. THE JAPANESE EMBASSY AND THE ZIPPER

Several weeks before Julie and David were to depart for Tokyo, Connie and I received an invitation from the Japanese Ambassador to a black tie dinner at the embassy. Like most such invitations that we were to receive over the years, it was addressed to *The Honorable Mr. and Mrs. Charles E. Stuart.* The use of the term "honorable" is a formal recognition of high office, but sometimes it seems to be prefixed to anyone of any consequence whatsoever. Even knowing of its overuse, I always enjoyed the compliment. Unlike some of our Washington colleagues, Connie and I tried to keep some perspective. If we were important at all, it was only because we worked for someone who was important.

Somehow, we learned that the meal would involve the use of chopsticks, a skill in which neither of us was proficient. We set about taking remedial chop-stick lessons by eating at Chinese restaurants prior to the dinner. I suppose we should have gone to Japanese eateries, but we didn't think the Ambassador would find out about our "disloyalty."

Because she had to be present at all social functions, day and night, at the White House, Connie had to take evening clothes to work on many occasions. She had a large and beautifully appointed corner office on the second floor of the East Wing. Here, she could safely change into evening wear before each event, apply makeup, and fix her hair in relative peace and quiet. This she did several nights a week, as the Nixons did a lot of entertaining. The men in the White House had access to the President's barber shop in the basement of the West Wing. There was no such facility for the ladies. Connie solved her time dilemma by letting her hair grow long and purchasing several hair pieces that she set at home when she needed a new "do."

On the night of the Japanese dinner, I took my tuxedo over to her office and we both changed. In the course of the transformation, she asked me to zip up the back of her gown. The zipper refused to go up. I tugged a little harder. Still no movement.

Garage mechanics say, "Don't force it. Get a bigger hammer." I applied this philosophy to the zipper, but it may not have been the right model to follow. I ripped the zipper out of the dress on one side. Notwithstanding its cost, it must have been of poor construction.

Connie was crestfallen. "You'll have to go without me," she wailed. "I can't do that," I responded. "Maybe Mrs. Nixon can fix you up." Connie proclaimed that she couldn't possibly call Mrs. Nixon and ask her for such assistance. I volunteered to place the call, as I was the cause of the problem. Mrs. Nixon told me to send Connie right up to the Family Quarters on the second floor. She had just finished getting Julie and David off to the Embassy. She could do us, too.

And so the wife of the President of the United States of America showed that in addition to being the First Lady, she was also qualified for another title. First Mother.

29. MOTORCADE MADNESS

Nixon's second foray behind the Iron Curtain was in 1970, to Belgrade, Yugoslavia. As with Bucharest the year before, the visit was widely hailed as a major step toward peace with the Warsaw Pact. Also, as with Bucharest, the city really put on a show for the visiting American President.

Huge throngs of cheering Yugoslavians lined the streets from the airport to Belgrade center. Marshal Tito, the head of state and head of government, was a perfect host. The crowds were so enthusiastic it was hard to remember we were visiting a Communist country. For 25 years these people had been persuaded that America was the enemy. Of course, as noted before, even in the US such crowds are created by professionals who know how to produce the desired result, but the faces seemed to reflect genuine pleasure and goodwill on the part of the public.

The motorcade dropped Mrs. Nixon and Connie off at a beautiful white marble structure simply referred to as "the Old Palace." Nixon and Tito went off to begin their bonding process at that ceremony which is *de rigueur* for visiting fireman and visiting Presidents, laying a wreath at the tomb of an unknown soldier.

The next morning the President left early to meet with Tito prior to leaving for Zagreb in the afternoon. Mrs. Nixon and Connie had an independent morning schedule consisting of a press reception and a visit to the "Pioneer Palace," before linking up with the President. The Pioneers are a sort of communist boy and girl scout organization, in red neckerchiefs.

Before the press reception ended, the motorcade began to form up in front of the Old Palace. The car for Mrs. Nixon and Mrs. Tito was a highly polished 1956 Cadillac, and the dozen or so security men, drivers and hangers-on all seemed quite proud of it. As is customary with motorcade management everywhere, the engines were left running as a precaution against the odd chance that they couldn't be restarted. It was a warm September morning and, after fifteen minutes or so of idling, telltale signs of white steam began to appear around the edges of the Caddy's hood. The driver, gesticulating wildly and babbling in dismay, opened the hood to find the radiator in an advanced state of overheating. This loss of cool quickly extended to the crowd of onlookers.

Watching the pandemonium with a mixture of sympathy and wonder, I considered whether I should intervene and help solve their problem. Most American men of my age had learned as teenagers that the cure for such a situation is to rev up the engine, so the fan draws increased air through the radiator and cools it down. However, that is a highly counter-intuitive measure to take and there was no way I could expect a translator to convince them it was safe. Alas, they did entirely the wrong thing. They turned the ignition off. Later, when they tried to restart the engine, it wouldn't turn over, as the hot metal had expanded. They had to push the Caddy out of line and move in a much less classy vehicle. The Yugoslavians were not rewarded for their efforts to create an atmosphere of sophistication. Unfortunately, it was not to be the only, nor the worst, of the motorcade problems that day.

The ultimate example of motorcade failure occurred at the Belgrade airport. As with so many problems in life, the essential cause was a failure to communicate. It is difficult enough when all parties speak the same language. It becomes virtually impossible when that is not the case. Not many Yugoslavians at that time spoke English, and fewer Americans were conversant in Serbian.

President Nixon and Marshall Tito had gone to Zagreb for the day. Nixon wanted to meet with the Croatian leaders. Tito wanted to ride on Air Force One and show Nixon his birthplace. As I wasn't needed on the trip, I spent the morning in the National Military Museum. I figured I would go out to the airport late in the afternoon and pick up Connie, who had traveled to Zagreb with the press. I would also be available in case there was anything I could do to help with the arrival. If ever an extra person could be useful with an arrival, this would be the time.

Sure enough, there were problems in Zagreb. Crowds and rain and Croatian leaders and cows on the runway and Lord knows what else had conspired to delay the travelers and the President arrived back in Belgrade two hours behind schedule. I had been sitting in a car at the airport for three hours when the President's 707 finally touched down. It had not been an uninteresting wait.

From my car, with a Yugoslavian driver (who claimed not to be proficient in English but who, given the times, might have been a counter espionage agent with a better command of the language than mine), I watched the motorcade form and reform fully three times before being put in some sort of order for the arrival. More cars kept arriving to be placed in one of the two lines that had been assembled beside the spot where the plane would park. Minor government officials who wanted to be able to brag that they were part of the arrival ceremony occupied some of the cars. Others, presumably belonging to officials who had gone to Zagreb, held only their drivers. They were all black Mercedes, and they all looked alike. When I got to 50, I stopped counting. There must have been close to 100 cars and 20 buses lined up on the tarmac. The motorcade's organizers, large teams of stocky men in ill-fitting suits, appeared to be charter subscribers to the doctrine: "when in danger or in doubt, run in circles, scream and shout."

To add to the difficulties, it had started to rain. Not an ordinary rain that permitted "running between the drops," but a torrential downpour that severely cut visibility in the growing dusk. Soon it was coming down in sheets, driven by a cold wind. The drivers of the cars and buses were reluctant to roll down their windows to hear instructions and certainly not willing to leave their vehicles to consult with bureaucrats. The Yugoslavians did not understand me or the Secret Service agents at the field. We did not understand them. And all of the translators were on aircraft returning from Zagreb. The sense of impending disaster soaked us like the rain.

When Air Force One landed, aides with umbrellas escorted Nixon and Tito to their cars. Due to the horizontal, driving nature of the rain, wet suits would have been more appropriate.

Then it happened. In a scene reminiscent of one of those old Oklahoma land rush photos, people streamed down the steps of Air Force One and raced to their cars. Or what they thought were their cars. Yugoslavs got in the cars meant for Americans and Americans got in cars meant for Yugoslavs. The drivers, not recognizing the strangers in their cars, protested vigorously in whatever language they had — which was all the more indecipherable since the speakers were so agitated. There were three people in cars meant for one and nobody in cars meant for two. There were people in both lines of cars, instead of just the one closest to the aircraft. The confusion was complete. Then, as I gazed, transfixed in horror, the motorcade began to move and uncoil like a great snake.

The original plan was that the secure portion of the motorcade, perhaps the front 20 cars, would leave first and the balance of the cars and all of the buses would wait for the other three 707s filled with Yugoslavians, White House staff and press corps, both domestic and international. At least, that is what the Yugoslavs had told us. That is not what happened.

By the time the lead security car reached the end of the tarmac it was probably doing fifty miles an hour. The rest of the cars, though apparently piloted by ex-racing drivers, were stretching out and the bus drivers were mashing gears and revving engines, trying to keep up. Soon the whole shooting match disappeared into the gloom of the gathering night. I was the sole American left and I had just inherited the problem of what to do with the three additional Boeing-loads of people which were beginning to land.

I called the Command Post and the Embassy Control Room and advised them of the situation. I told them to put someone on duty getting the empty buses to return. I wasn't concerned about the car for the third assistant to the Deputy Minister for Hog Production. I wanted the buses for the press and staff, both of whom became easily annoyed and had ready venues for expressing their grievances.

Belgrade airport is not Chicago O'Hare. Its resources had been taxed with Air Force One. There were no jetways, of course, and apparently a limited number of rolling steps. I was having difficulty in finding ground crew willing to brave the rain to find a way to unload the planes. Of course, even if I had found steps for every plane, there was still no place to go. We were at the edge of the field, far away from the terminal, and it was still raining. The passengers would simply have to wait on board their aircraft for the buses to return.

Then, just as I was beginning to acquire some facility in sign language, I got a call on my radio. It was the White House Command Post, a secure room operated by the Secret Service and WHCA and equipped with the radio base station.

"Stuart, Stuart. This is Belgrade Base. What is your location? Over." "Base, base, this is Stuart. I am still at the airport. Over." "Stuart, Mr. Chapin just called and informed us that Searchlight's (the Presidents code name) tuxedo is on aircraft tail number 8970 and he needs it immediately for the State Dinner beginning in two hours. Can you get it and take it to the guesthouse. Over?"

"Base, this is Stuart. Affirmative. Will deliver Tux to Searchlight. Stuart out."
"Base out." What the hell. I didn't have any other crises to cope with.

With much gesticulation and pointing, I managed to get a set of steps to the edge of the field and 8970. I boarded the airplane and briefed the pilot on the situation. I asked him to contact the other aircraft and told him that I had informed the Embassy control staff and assured him that people were working on securing ground transportation. Sooner or later, things would be straightened out. Then I took the tuxedo, picked up my wife and "got out of Dodge," much relieved that a higher priority had come along before I — as the last man standing, as it were — could be blamed for the fiasco. The passengers wanted to get off the planes and were growing restless. (They were destined to grow a lot more restless. It would be three hours later when the last of them got back to their hotels.)

There was only one positive aspect to an otherwise calamitous day. Dan Rather, a Nixon nemesis, was the CBS reporter who covered the White House in those days. He had missed the return flight. He was still in Zagreb.

30. Olympic Gold

Query. If presidents dream of other goals or Walter Mitty lives, of what do they dream? What could a man who has fulfilled the ambition of so many little boys in America possibly want?

In the case of Richard Nixon, other than Republican control of Congress, or at the least the power to line item veto, my guess is that he would have wished for greater athletic prowess. Nixon was a frustrated football player.

When he was a young man at Whittier College, a small Quaker school in California and hardly a football powerhouse, he regularly went out for the team. Just as regularly, he occupied a seat at the end of the bench. Nonetheless, in speeches during his presidency, Nixon frequently referred to Whittier's football coach, "Coach Newman," as being one of the major influences on his life. His disappointment at not being a better athlete was clear to a discerning listener.

He kept up his interest in football through the rest of his life. As president, he became the Washington Redskins' First Fan. He even dreamed up new plays and sent them to George Allen, the Redskin's coach. This must have caused some consternation on Allen's part. Should he go for the coach's hall of fame, directing his players as he knew best, or cater to the First Fan and feature an amateur's idea of a clever play on national television?

When the White House was able to attract Bud Wilkinson, the legendary football coach at Oklahoma in the 50s and 60s, to be the head of the President's Council on Physical Fitness, Nixon was as proud as if he had gotten a first round draft choice. Bud was one of those men who was simply so nice that it was hard to see how he had become such a great coach. In a profession that tends to rely on strong temper and a willingness to use it, he was an outstanding exception.

At any rate, Nixon knew that sports figures were the heroes of the time. Partly in view of this, he became fixated on getting the Olympic Games to the United States in the year of our bicentennial, 1976.

The President's schedule is fairly proscribed, being packed with timed meetings and events. A typical day might start with, 8:00 AM, meeting with the national security advisor; 9:00 AM, presentation of credentials, new ambassador from Liberia; 9:20 AM, photo session in Rose Garden with poster child for March of Dimes. For this reason, whenever he and Bob Haldeman had an opportunity to think together in a relaxed, hands-behind-the-head fashion, it was generally an unscheduled opportunity that came along. It at was at such times that they occasionally sent for me. I do not recall ever having an appointment in advance to meet with the President. True to fashion, one day in early 1970, I received a call from Haldeman asking if I could join him in the President's office as they had something to discuss with me. Bob Haldeman was a bright fellow and was not given to asking idle questions; at least he was polite enough to couch such a command in gentle terms.

When I arrived at the Oval Office, Bob explained that later that year, the International Olympic Committee (IOC) was meeting in Amsterdam to select the site of the 1976 games. Two American cities were bidding: Los Angeles for the summer games and Denver for the winter. (The summer and winter games have since been scheduled two years apart.) The President was interested in having both games in 1976, the nation's bicentennial. He was captivated by the thought of having the summer games in California, his home state, as he would undoubtedly be invited to participate in some way or could better control events.

I was to be appointed as a special presidential emissary to render assistance to the US Olympic Committee. I would start by participating in a trip to the Nordic countries, culminating at Holmenkollen, the Norwegian winter ski jumping festival. The trip was being organized by the Los Angeles Olympic Committee and was leaving that very weekend. Bob then informed me that the State Department was in the process of issuing me a diplomatic passport. (When we traveled overseas on presidential trips, the Department of State just collected all of our personal passports at the beginning of the trip and handed them back on the way home.)

The President told me that it was very important to him that the games be in LA and that I should do whatever I could to achieve that goal. Bob gave me the name of the head of the LA committee, Jim Kilroy, who turned out to be a delightful fellow as well as a long time supporter of the President. He also gave me the name of a contact at the State Department. That was it. Talk about *A Message to Garcia*. I had a lot to do in very short order.

When I got back to my office I called "our man at State" and arranged for a meeting the next morning to educate me on the Olympics. At the time, I knew little more than which TV network carried them.

I soon learned that the Olympics were operated by an organization called the International Olympic Committee, the members of which were representatives of each of the countries that participated in the games. These people, as I came to know them, were a group of confirmed internationalists, usually wealthy, sometimes former athletes, often imperious, always political, adult males who were used to being treated like royalty. In fact, I met one who *was* royalty, King Constantine of Greece. These people traveled around the world on other people's money and were lavished with attention (until the scandal in Salt Lake City), feted, entertained and generally treated like rock stars by cities vying to be selected as hosts for the games in six years time. The selection was made at a spring festival, in a secret vote. If this election did not generate the same degree of suspense as waiting for the smoke at St. Peter's, it was not for want of trying

The man from State informed me that three cities were competing for the summer games, Los Angeles, Moscow and Montreal. He had prepared a list of member countries of the IOC. He had also forecast how they might cast their votes, based upon historical and current political relationships.

From the very beginning he believed that the contest was between Moscow and Los Angeles. The world's two largest economic powers, two largest military powers and two largest political powers were going to slug it out. Poor little Montreal was probably going to only get the votes of England and some of the Commonwealth countries. Moscow could count on the votes of Warsaw Pact nations. The US could rely on the votes of its allies. The rest of the world would vote for either Los Angeles or Moscow, depending on the politics of the time. At least, that's what our Department of State figured.

When I attended the gala voting convention in Amsterdam in the spring of 1970, I was amazed at how *badly* the countries wanted the games. It was not because they were profitable. At the time, the last city that had financially broken even was Los Angeles in 1928. The Amsterdam equivalent of the Washington Convention Center was filled with displays, audio-video projections, literature and enough stunning models to stock the Detroit Auto show. Moscow had printed a beautiful hard cover, four-color book with captioning in four languages. Their people made the point, to anyone who would listen, that Los Angeles had already hosted the games. Now it should be Moscow's turn. Meanwhile, I was telling the delegates that President Nixon *really* wanted the games during the year of celebration of our Declaration of Independence. I was passing out presidential tie clips to anyone who was not wearing a dashiki. The Republican National Convention came to mind; much of the dynamics were the same.

After several days of P&P (partying and politicking), the delegates sequestered themselves for the secret vote while the rest of the throng did whatever they could to mask the strain of waiting for the announcement. No matter how many times we forecast the votes, the Moscow/Los Angeles competition was too close to call. We were all nervous.

In 1976, the year of the American Bicentennial, the summer Olympic games were held in Montreal, Canada. As we have since learned with the ice skating scandal in 2002, there is a certain amount of deal making between Olympic judges. Apparently, such was the case between members of the IOC in 1970. All of the small countries of the world voted for Montreal, choosing neutral ground and voting for the underdog. They were afraid of being caught between the jaws of the world's largest nutcracker, the USSR and the USA.

I telephoned Bob Haldeman right after the vote and reported the failure of my first diplomatic mission. At least, he was the one who had to give the bad news to the President.

31. PRESIDENTIAL LARGESSE

Presidents, all presidents, enjoy dispensing gifts to visitors to the Oval Office. Sometimes the presents have personal connotations and significance as, for example, President Kennedy's PT 109 tie bars or Ike's monogrammed golf balls. Most of the time, however, it is just ordinary stuff enhanced with the addition of a Presidential Seal. Anything you can use in daily life becomes more valuable with the addition of the Seal of the President of the United States. This is his seal; only he is allowed to use it. There are even penalties for reproducing it without White House permission. (When I worked for John Ehrlichman, we were petitioned by a book publisher to use the seal in a design for a dust jacket. We refused.)

President Johnson emblazoned everything in sight with the seal. He may well have ordered that his personal toothbrush be so defined. All presidents order cufflinks, tie bars, charms, pins, paperweights, letter openers, pens and assorted jewelry in varying degrees of value. The cheap ball point pens are meant to be handed out by advance men to people who have been helpful; solid silver or gold cuff links are for higher ups. All of this I learned from a genial gentleman named Frank Shoaf, representing the Balfour Jewelry Company, shortly after I arrived in the White House. Balfour had been suppliers of jewelry items to previous presidents. How Mr. Shoaf had been directed to me, I never ascertained. But presidential gift selection became another part of my job.

I do not know about other presidents, but Nixon and Haldeman, with an involvement bordering on micro management, were keenly interested in my choices. From time to time I would be asked to appear in the Oval Office to display the wares that various companies had sent to the White House. Such items were directed to me for disposition.

There is no formal recognition of suppliers to the White House as there is in England, i.e. "purveyors to her Majesty the Queen." Notwithstanding this lack of distinction, there are always some manufacturers trying to get their products introduced to the president personally. These companies would send samples ranging from glassware to neckties to framed documents. When I went to Oval Office with these trade goods, I always felt a little like a jewelry peddler, laying out various items on the broad expanse of the President's desk and discussing the alternative costs. "Mr. President, this can be ordered in gold for $X, or gold wash for $Y. Which would you prefer?"

These trinkets were rarely charged to the president. He had a White House operating account which paid for most of the stuff. The Republican Party was charged if the items were for political purposes, the Department of State if foreign visitors were to be the recipients.

I kept the new sample items in a credenza behind my desk. I did not bother to lock this cabinet, under the assumption that the White House was a pretty secure place. Apparently, I was wrong. Once, after I had been out of the office for a full week on a trip, my secretary Nancy Woodruff, a dear and serious soul, approached me with what was, to her, an alarming story.

Nancy, being dutiful and protective, one morning in my absence noticed some papers on my desk had been disturbed and explored further. She opened the credenza and found that several gift items were missing. She promptly locked the credenza and called the Secret Service. In short order the incident worked its way up to the head of the Technical Services Division (TSD), a very competent agent named Al Wong, who proceeded to design a trap. He ordered the construction of a false vent at the juncture of wall and ceiling opposite the credenza. He then hung a large clock on another wall. He placed a security camera in the vent with a motorized panning action, sweeping the room from the door to the clock to the credenza. He would not only catch the perpetrator on tape, he would know exactly what time it was. This was all accomplished within 24 hours of Nancy's report. Even petty theft is taken seriously at the White House.

The very next night the thief returned. He entered into the room when the camera was panning the credenza. He walked across the floor when the camera was panning the clock. He bent over the credenza with his back to the camera.

His entire visit was recorded, but Al never got a facial shot or even enough of the body to identify him.

At night the White House and EOB are alive with guards, floor cleaners, smudge removers, painters, handymen, light bulb changers, and clock winders. The thief was one of the minions who had passed security clearance — he was not a foreign agent or a risk to the life of the President. Clearly, however, he had not been vetted for potential tie bar theft. The trap was kept baited for another week or so after I returned, but the thief never reappeared. It was then quietly dismantled. It required an agent to sit and run through the entire eight-hour tape that, even when speeded up, required considerable time to view. The Secret Service's advice to Nancy and me was to keep the credenza locked.

Sometimes the simplest solutions are the best.

32. Leaving the White House

In the summer of 1968, before I joined the Administration, before there *was* a Nixon Administration, I read *The Ordeal of Power* by Emmit John Hughes. He observed that the average tenure of a White House staff member was 19 months. At the time, I really didn't think much about that statistic. Like most people around the country and away from Washington, I really didn't think about the White House staff much at all. I was highly concerned about the party affiliation of its occupant, but it ended there. I knew who the press secretary was and the chief of staff and maybe one or two other familiar names. The staff, its makeup and functions were unknown and largely uninteresting. This was to change dramatically when John Ehrlichman asked me to become his principal assistant. I started work the Monday following the election at the transition office and remained on the job an average of twelve hours a day until 7 April 1971, when I left.

The position was always exciting. Up until I separated, I always got a thrill, a palpable tingle, when I turned in to park on West Executive Drive and entered the White House grounds. During the whole first year, I was convinced I would stay for the duration, including a second term if there was one. I left even before the first term was over, although I beat the average by nearly a year.

I left for a variety of reasons. It was only after considerable soul searching and analysis that I told Bob Haldeman that I would be leaving as soon as I found another position. He asked me to consider staying in the Administration but in another role. Perhaps I would consider a department or agency? He offered to help something open up. I said I would consider any job that he might come up with but I knew in my heart of hearts that nothing would be as rewarding or glamorous as the job I was giving up. So why was I leaving?

The principal consideration was that I was still a young man and needed to get back to the business world. With the campaign, the transition and White House staff I had devoted about as much time as I felt I could spare from my career. Traveling around the world on Air Force One was exciting, but it was not adding to my business skills. I did not aspire to become a Washington "rep" or lobbyist, as did so many of my colleagues. Further, not being an attorney, I could not look forward to joining a Washington law firm. Most importantly, I was in politics because of Richard Nixon and not as a career. Real estate development was a field that seemed interesting to me and I thought that, if I were to obtain a position in that business, I had better get started.

There was also the consideration of the upcoming campaign for reelection. As a hunter, I know that during the rut, deer go wild in the woods. After my experience in 1968, I have held the view that the quadrennial election cycle was the "political rutting season." I had been through one and really didn't want to go through another.

Also, I was growing tired of the pace. I had breakfast every morning at 7:00 AM in the White House Navy Mess. I rarely left for home before 7:00 in the evening. I was traveling all the time and was absent from home a great deal. I had very little time to myself.

When you work personally for the president, his schedule comes before yours. Your have no social life of your own. The little things in life, like balancing the checkbook, taking the suits to the cleaners and mowing the lawn, become difficult. Some people had spouses who could take care of this minutia but, in my case, we were both tails on the same kite. Connie was working even longer hours and traveling more than I was. Further, I had a number of hobbies and interests that I was neglecting and wanted to pursue.

Lastly, the artificial and self-imposed pressures were getting to me. The White House is under the microscope of the world. There is a press corps of several thousand just watching for mistakes, any mistakes. Moreover, my immediate boss, Bob Haldeman, was the chief proponent of the zero-defects movement. I was wearying of the game.

On April 2, 1971, I penned the following letter to Richard Nixon:

THE WHITE HOUSE

WASHINGTON

My Dear Mr. President:

On completing his sojourn at Walden pond, Henry David Thoreau noted: "I left the woods for as good a reason as I went there. Perhaps it seemed to me that I had several more lives to live and could not spare any more time for that one." Thoreau's words have great personal meaning to me at this time of my leaving your service for an exceptional opportunity in private industry.

Like Thoreau's two years at Walden, my two years on the White House staff have been the most fulfilling of my life. When, in January, 1968, I began working as a volunteer in your New York campaign headquarters, I did not even dream of the "high adventure" which you were later to describe in your inaugural address; and yet, for me, that is an apt description of my experience as a member of your staff. Now, on the eve of my departure, I want you to know that I will always treasure that adventure and that, whatever else I may do with my career, I shall always look upon the past two years as a highpoint in my life. Know too that I will always be available if I can be of further help.

My best personal wishes to you, Sir.

Yours sincerely,

Charles E. Stuart

I received the following response:

THE WHITE HOUSE

WASHINGTON

May 14, 1971

Dear Chuck:

The very thoughtful letter you sent to me on your departure from the White House expresses the same spirit that has meant so much to our progress during these past three years. If it is true, as I believe, that the greatest satisfaction in life comes from working in a cause greater than oneself, your contribution to our Administration's efforts has proven as valuable to you as it has to me.

Your readiness to take on the awkward challenge, to solve the difficult problem and to do so with distinction, has made an important difference in our achievements. You know how grateful I am for your help, but I want to take this opportunity to express my personal thanks to you once again. In whatever you may undertake, the best wishes of all the Nixons will go with you throughout the years ahead.

Sincerely,

Richard Nixon

Over the years, when I have been asked what I did at the White House, I have responded that I was an "odd job man, a utility outfielder." Was I involved in the creation of major new domestic policy? No, I was not. Nor was I consulted on great and serious decisions or foreign policy matters. I did not help to end the Vietnam war.

I was kept very busy with a series of small matters that mostly had to do with politics, the operation of the White House, the President's personal life and that of his family. The most important and satisfying reward for me was that I had the President's confidence. He entrusted me with his wife and children and knew that I would not let them get into any trouble. He sent for me when there was a job to be done which involved judgment or discretion. I think he liked me. That was enough.

33. WATERGATE

Richard Nixon once said that "timing in politics was everything." I concur with this statement, but expand it to "timing in life is everything." I left the White House when Watergate was just the name of a hotel and office building. (Ironically, I was hired for my next job at the Watergate, where my future employer maintained a suite of offices.) Had I stayed much longer, I probably would have been drawn into the reelection campaign in a senior position. Many individuals who would never have sanctioned breaking and entering, or other forms of blatant criminal behavior, were caught up in the furor and numerous conspiracy charges injured or destroyed many of my friends. Just knowing about such activities or being present in meetings when certain things were discussed was enough to cause an indictment.

The Pentagon Papers were a multi-volume collection of studies of the Vietnam War produced by the Rand Corporation. They were Top Secret, as they contained numerous plain English copies of messages that were originally sent in code. US intelligence agencies, the CIA, DIA, NSA, and others, had rooms full of recorded tapes of coded Russian messages waiting to be broken. It was assumed that the Soviets had similar stockpiles of recordings of US radio transmissions. In addition to other security and political considerations, the *Pentagon Papers* would swerve as the key enabling them to break some of these codes, a sort of a modern Rosetta stone. There was also a great deal of other secret information in the *Papers*.

Daniel Ellsberg, the grandson of a highly distinguished American naval officer, was, like Krogh, a zealot in a narrow area. He was convinced that the US government had erred in its conduct of the war. He felt that it was his patriotic duty to release the facts; and he gave the *Pentagon Papers* to *The New York Times*. The US Department of Justice promptly filed a lawsuit against him.

In the more than a quarter of a century that has passed since "Watergate," there has been a general blurring of the events that comprised this American tragedy. The original sin was breaking into the Democratic Headquarters in order to plant listening devices. The accused mastermind of this action was G. Gordon Liddy. (Not to be considered an amelioration of this incursion of privacy, and for information only: Lyndon Johnson routinely ordered electronic spying on Barry Goldwater in 1964 and on Richard Nixon in 1968. The Nixon campaign, knowing this, employed a retired FBI agent to "sweep" the hotel rooms at every stop.

Nixon had been putting pressure on Chuck Colson to get information on the Chairman of the Democratic Party, Larry O'Brian, and his work as a secret lobbyist for the eccentric millionaire, Howard Hughes. Colson, in turn, pressured his staff. "Stuff flows downhill." Ultimately, G. Gordon Liddy was presented with the problem of getting the goods on O'Brian. Liddy proved to be an eager recipient of such requests. He promptly organized a wire tapping expedition at the Watergate.

The breaking into the psychiatrist's office of Daniel Ellsberg, organized by Bud Krogh and David Young of the "Plumbers" (and ultimately laid at the feet of John Ehrlichman) was also wrong, but Bud was a zealot willing to break the law in order to safeguard "law and order." To that characteristic must be added abundant but misguided patriotism.

The "Plumbers" (so named because they stopped leaks) were given the task of getting the background on Ellsberg. As Ellsberg was known to have some weird habits, including potential drug use, the plumbers thought they might gain some information from his psychiatrist's files. This they would use in the trial to incriminate or, at the very least, discredit him. The primary mission of the US Government is the defense of the homeland and keeping the citizenry safe; the paradoxical question is, at what point does such overblown "defense" actually destroy the liberty that is the cherished basis of American life? To these men, the illegal entering of the psychiatrist's office was justified; and if the United States had a version of England's *Official Secrets Act*, Ellsberg, who had sworn an oath not to reveal secrets, would have gone to jail. Directly, "without passing go."

In the case of Ellsberg, Richard Nixon was leading the parade of those upset by the release of the papers. He was keen that Ellsberg be found guilty. This intense interest on the part of the President energized people, including Krogh, to the point where they did things they would have considered condemnable under other circumstance. There was quite some controversy at the time over whether they were criminals or heroes.

The "Dirty Tricks" department of Donald Segretti and Dwight Chapin also generated some public sympathy at the same time they were condemned. Obstructing that sacrosanct "democratic process" that Americans believe they enjoy is, indeed, wrong, but on the face of it, they merely sprang a number of schoolboy pranks. The two men went to jail for heinous crimes such as sending 200 pizza pies to a Democratic dinner and loosing white mice at a Muskie press conference. Their most serious stunt was interfering with the Democratic primary in Florida. Segretti sent out broadsides on Muskie stationery, accusing an opponent of having an illegitimate child. Other mailings accused Hubert Humphrey of having a drunk driving citation and Senator Jackson of being a homosexual.

Defamatory mailings are reprehensible and dishonesty in attribution is, too. However, libelous, untrue attacks are a part of American political history. They have happened to nearly every Presidential candidate. In early times it was the opposition press, such as the *Aurora*, with its campaign against John Adams, or the New York *World*, spreading fabrications about Abraham Lincoln. With Segretti, it was direct mail. Today, it is the Internet. Even the illegitimate child stunt has been tried before. (In President Cleveland's case, it was true.)

My own involvement with another "Watergate" incident caused me to be summoned to testify before the Grand Jury.

During the transition, President Johnson, who had known Nixon for a long, long time and rather liked him, invited him to visit at the White House for a day. (On a trip to Thailand, I am told, President Johnson was asked by the Prince of that country about the difference between Humphrey and Nixon. Johnson, an earthy man, reached across and grasped the startled monarch by the testicles. Johnson proclaimed that "Nixon has balls." During the course of conversation, Johnson, who was motivated by a number of things in life, not the least of which were women and money, apparently asked Nixon about his vice presidential papers. Johnson then described how he had just donated his own vice presidential files to the US Archives for a very large tax deduction as a charitable contribution. Nixon latched onto the concept, although he was hardly as rapacious as Johnson. He got the name of the appraiser who evaluated Johnson's papers. (And, Nixon was not motivated by the ladies.)

When he got back to New York, the President-elect requested John Ehrlichman to have all the many cartons holding his vice presidential papers appraised and to make arrangements to donate them to the Archives. They were stored in a warehouse leased by Nixon, Mudge, Rose, Guthry, Alexander, and Mitchell, Nixon's law firm. As John later described it, the appraiser from Chicago "opened a few boxes, sprinkled a little holy water around and left." He appraised them at a very high value. John then turned the remainder of the assignment over to me.

Shortly after we arrived in Washington, I contacted the General Services Administration and the US Archives. I made arrangements to have the boxes picked up in New York and trucked to Washington. An additional archivist was engaged with the specific responsibility of organizing the Nixon vice presidential papers. The young man selected for the position was sent over to meet me and get any exact direction the White House desired. There being none, I promptly put the whole incident out of my mind.

A year later the US Congress enacted legislation that prohibited Federal officers from donating papers accumulated while in government service back to the government for a tax deduction. After all, the documents were developed at taxpayer expense; it's hard to make a case that the country should have to pay, via tax breaks, to get them back. Nixon's papers were donated before the law was changed. However, when Nixon's tax accountant learned of the rules change, he realized there was no formal paper trail and there was no deed presenting the documents to the Archives. So, a deed was prepared, backdated and signed by my old friend Edward Morgan. During the Watergate investigation this falsehood was discovered and was listed as yet another of the many dubious acts of which Nixon was accused.

Perhaps no deed was even needed. The papers had been in the Archives for over a year. I delivered them, myself. Nor was there any legitimate doubt about their being a gift, nor any doubt that they were of value. I explained all of this to the Grand Jury. I pleaded with them to recognize that no crime had been committed. There was no looting of the Treasury. However, in the highly charged atmosphere of the time, the grand jury exhibited all the bloodlust of the citizen's courts of the French Revolution. The backdating of the deed was considered a breach of the law. Ed Morgan was disbarred and went to jail. He never fully recovered and his brilliant professional future was never realized.

There is one other incident which gives some perspective on the times.

Among the many incidents that made up "Watergate" was the charge that Richard Nixon used the taxpayer's money to improve his western home, *Casa Pacifica*. Indeed, this may have been done, but not by Nixon.

As I have related, the presidency is an awe inspiring office. All of the employees of the US Government are subject to its spell. The military officer who ordered backups on backups in Bangkok was a precursor of some General Services Administration manager. This poor fellow was instructed by the Secret Service to plant some shrubs at *Casa Pacifica* in order to provide some visual screening. He took it upon himself to order a landscaping upgrade of the whole house. The Secret Service installed a security system. The Navy put in a flagpole. These, to my knowledge, were the items that were trumpeted as examples of Nixon using federal funds to improve his home.

Following is a memorandum that Nixon wrote to John Ehrlichman *before* he was inaugurated, regarding his desire to use personal funds for home improvements.

January 4, 1969

TO: JOHN EHRLICHMAN

FROM   RN

RE: SUMMER RESIDENCE

I have decided against having the Marine Corps build a summer residence for the President at Camp Pendleton.

There are two options which I would like explored. The first is to find some separately isolated house that I could personally buy somewhere below Laguna and above Oceanside. In that way we could use the Marine Corps Base for a landing field and have rather quick access to the property.

On reflection, while I would like to have this house on the beach, I realize that privacy in such a crowded area might be very difficult. If one could be found within 5 or 10 minutes driving time from a good beach this might serve the purpose. What I suggest is that the Marine Corps make available a good swimming beach on their property and then I purchase a home which is not too far away from it.

A second possibility — which would probably present insurmountable legal problems — would be for me to build a modest residence upon Marine Corps property and on the beach and then give the house to the government.

My major concern is the unfavorable publicity that might accrue if we allow a very expensive residence to be constructed by the Marine Corps. The armed services are wasting money, on a very extravagant basis around the world, and I am going to urge Laird to cut into this waste on a massive basis. I can't do that on the one hand and then have the Marine Corps build a residence for me at the same time.

The handling of Key Biscayne I think has been proper up to this point. I am putting out all the money to buy the property and, of course, will pay for the redecoration, etc. All that the government will provide is the helicopter pad and a place to land a boat. Both of these actions in the long run will save money because of the need for additional security in the event that I used a public boat landing or a helicopter pad which was not adjacent to the residence.

For purposes of PR you ought to get the exact figures on how much money the government has invested in the facilities at the LBJ ranch. I think landing strip, roads and other buildings they have constructed there should amount to something near three million dollars. There is also the immense amount of office space that he has in Austin. I want you to get me a complete run down on what has been spent for Johnson and have this available for Klein and others in the event that any columnists are raising questions about the very modest amounts that are being spent for me.

In this connection, as you are probably aware, Eisenhower's El Dorado house was given to him by friends and the same is true of the place that was made available to him at Augusta.

Let's just be sure that since I am being extremely careful to avoid milking the public treasury that we get the proper credit or at least avoid discredit.

As far as the residence in California is concerned, I would be willing to put up $150,000 to $200,000. It would be my plan to sell the property which I own on Whittier Boulevard in which my Mother lived and to reinvest that into this property. What is probably needed here is a very discreet personal friend who will roam around that area and find a good place which we can purchase near the Marine beach property. What we might find is that we should take a house that may have the basic requirements as far as plumbing, etc. are concerned which might require remodeling. From a political standpoint I am very anxious to work out a deal on this as soon as we can find the right property. I don't like the idea of being a Florida resident and while we will allow this situation to go on for about a year because of various considerations, at an appropriate time I think the California residence will become my domicile for all purposes, tax and otherwise."

This concern for taxpayer money was in stark contrast to his predecessor. The White House military office has a way of discreetly funding things that presidents want to accomplish. Johnson considered the fund to be his private bank. During the time I was at the White House, the fund was administered by Bill Gully, a retired Marine gunnery sergeant. According to "Gully", more than $3,000,000 was spent on improvements at the Johnson ranch. In the mid 1960s, this was a lot of money.

The Army general in charge of the White House Communications Agency once told me that Lyndon Johnson had taken him by the arm and showed him a site on the LBJ ranch. Johnson then told him it was a fine site for a building in which to store radio equipment. When the General protested, "Mr. President, I don't need a place to store equipment," Johnson told him that he didn't understand. The ranch needed a cattle barn and the DOD was going to build it. The taxpayers thus constructed the only army radio storage facility in the country that looked like a cattle barn.

As I suspect is the case with all former Nixon staff, I have been asked many, many times about the break-in. Do I think Nixon ordered it? Do I think he knew about it in advance?

My answer to both of these questions has always been "No." I certainly do not believe that President Nixon ordered a breaking and entering of the headquarters of the Democratic National Committee at the Watergate Hotel. Nor do I believe he knew about it in advance. Nothing that I have read would lead me to believe that. I do believe that Nixon learned about the connection between the break-in and his reelection committee before the rest of us did.

Most likely, Nixon thought that it would all quickly blow over; that the Watergate break-in was just the action of another overeager campaign worker (as it was, of course) of the type he had seen so many of in his long career in politics. When the matter didn't vanish promptly, he began to deny the activity in order to protect his own people. It was the cover-up that destroyed him.

And what are my thoughts on the "threats" exposed on the Nixon tapes, i.e. "We should firebomb Brookings"?

Who among us has never been so angered at another person's actions that we have said something like, "I could kill him/her for that!" In a fit of pique, people say things that they know will actually not happen and that they do not actually mean. However, when Nixon said such things, some of his support people didn't know he was just blowing off steam; they took action. This is my explanation for some of what happened in Watergate and what makes the tapes sound so criminally conspiratorial. Bob Haldeman was subjected to many such outrageous comments and took them as such, not as directives. Unfortunately, when Nixon made comments like these to Colson and others, they saluted and said, "Yes sir."

Watergate was a story that moved with exponential acceleration. Reporters across the country began to investigate every nuance of Nixon's Presidency. They uncovered items such as the Vice Presidential papers and *Casa Pacifica*. Under other circumstances, many of these episodes would have been accepted as relatively innocuous, but now, they were turned into critical stories. The headline writers were in competition with each other. And suddenly, it was too late. Nixon had lost the good will and best wishes of the public. His Presidency was beyond repair.

The collection of incidents called "Watergate" ironically supports those leaders who prefer to control everything personally. It is exceedingly difficult to select staff who are self-starters but who are not inclined to become free agents, who are reliable in their judgment and can be counted on not to overstep the law. Enthusiasm and devotion to a cause can easily spill over to fanaticism and excess, and some people think "all's fair" if it will be helpful to the "cause," whatever that may be.

Watergate also taught the lesson that it is mighty hard to cover up bad behavior.

I left the White House staff in April 1971, before Watergate. Much has been written about it all by individuals who have more insight and facts than I. However, I have shared some background on several of the elements with which I have some familiarity.

34. THOUGHTS ON DEEP THROAT

The former Deputy Director of the Federal Bureau of Investigation, Mark Felt, made the startling revelation on May 31, 2005, that he was the source who anonymously "leaked" the Pentagon Papers to the newspapers, betraying the President, his boss. His disclosure answered one disturbing question in one of the greatest controversies of the era.

As a former White House staffer, I am presumed to know something about Deep Throat. I possessed no inside information, but it always seemed to me that Fred Fielding was the most likely suspect. Even Bob Haldeman told me (during my visit with him at Lompoc prison) that he thought it was Fielding.

I don't remember ever having met Mr. Fielding, but his position in the White House made him a much more likely candidate than most of the others who were named as potential suspects. As John Dean's assistant, he had access to the information that was developed in Dean's investigations of the complex story of the break ins (Watergate and Daniel Ellsberg's psychiatrist's office), the Plumbers, Chuck Colson, Gordon Liddy, Howard Hunt, et al. Also, as a recent addition to the staff, he was not a long-time Nixon loyalist as was Leonard Garment, another White House attorney who had been suggested as a possible teller of tales. I knew Len Garment. He had been Nixon's law partner in New York. He would never have turned against his friend. I also knew Alexander Haig, long considered a prime suspect. He has too strong a sense of honor to turn informer. None of the others who were commonly named as possible Deep Throats held jobs that would have acquainted them with the full range of facts.

In retrospect, knowing something about J. Edgar Hoover, I should have placed a bet on Felt. I didn't. I thought Hoover was a one-of-a-kind in his abuse of power at the FBI, an aberration. But he wasn't. The genes were passed on.

Hoover was a phenomenon in Washington. He lasted through successive administrations, going on and on like the Energizer bunny. He gave new meaning to the expression, "knowledge is power." Hoover sought to ingratiate himself with, or outright blackmail, everyone of consequence in Washington. He placed particular emphasis on presidents and members of the Congress who had any relationship, budgetary or oversight, with the Bureau. He did this by using information vacuumed up by his loyal agents.

This is how Hoover's FBI worked. A new congressman would arrive in town. If it appeared that he would remain for more than a term, Hoover would find something to show him. "Congressman, one of my agents was conducting an investigation at the University of_____ regarding a criminal matter. He just happened to take this photograph of a student anti-war rally. In the second row is a girl with her shirt off, carrying a sign 'Make love, not war.' When I realized the girl was your daughter, I ordered the negative destroyed. I am giving you the only print." Thus, J. Edgar would have another "friend" in the House of Representatives, ready to call on if the need arose. He had incriminating material, real or fabricated, on many public figures; and he had no hesitancy to blackmail the lawmakers over their own peccadilloes.

The FBI was notorious for its "black bag" jobs (illegal entry) that provided electronic surveillance, phone taps, etc., ordered by Hoover. His actions against the Black leader Dr. Martin Luther King are well documented. Hoover recorded King's romantic trysts in various hotel rooms and carted the tapes to the Oval Office. There, he and President Johnson humorously shared the knowledge of the sexual exploits of a man whom neither of them respected. Hoover came to New York to visit Nixon at the transition office to cement relations with the new President. He did not bring the King tapes with him. The strait-laced Nixon would not have found them entertaining.

When Hoover died in May of 1973, Nixon attended the funeral. Perhaps under the dictum *de mortuis nil nisi bonum*, he said only positive things about the man. Most of official Washington probably just breathed a sigh of relief.

After decades of evidence, most people knew to be wary of Hoover; it would have been a mistake of the first order of magnitude on Nixon's part to elevate Felt to the Director's position he coveted so much. Felt, as Hoover's

Deputy, had been steeped in the marinade of intrigue for the preservation of personal power.

Felt's claim that he was Deep Throat refutes his standing as a loyal FBI agent. Some in the media have tried to make a hero out of Felt by portraying him as a "whistleblower." They are trying to convince the public, most of whom know Watergate only as a Presidential scandal of some sort, that Felt acted bravely, that he was an honest man caught in a conflict, that he did the "right thing." That is simply not the case.

Felt was not some mid-level bureaucrat at the DOD going public about failures in a new weapons system. He was one of the nation's highest-ranking law enforcement officers. He had an absolute obligation to keep confidential any information obtained through investigation. He had the same requirement for secrecy as a member of a grand jury. (The Watergate Grand Jury proceedings also became known to the public on a daily basis, but more through leaks from the staff than through jury members.) Citizens of the United States, from the insignificant to the mighty, must have confidence that government officials will not publicly reveal information about them acquired during an investigation.

Further, if he felt there was an inappropriate cover-up taking place, he had other options. He was the deputy director of an office in the US Department of Justice. Above him in rank were the Attorney General, the Deputy Attorney General and a slew of Assistant and Deputy Assistant Attorneys General. He could have gone to one of them and filed a complaint. If this were done, if a formal internal action were filed, on the record, matters would have come to a head. An investigation would have been undertaken. Or, if he was unsure what kind of repercussions would follow the filing of such a complaint with Nixon appointees, he could have gone to the Congressional Committee with oversight over the FBI. Either way, the facts would have come out in the end.

Instead, Mr. Felt, weaned in the school of J. Edgar Hoover and bitter about being passed over for promotion, went to *The Washington Post* as an anonymous source. Unlike a true "whistleblower," Felt didn't even have the courage to go public in his own name.

35. The Funeral

Richard M. Nixon, the only president of the United States to resign, spent his last years rebuilding his reputation, an effort in which he was largely successful. He became an elder statesman of note. When he passed away on April 22, 1994, it was a major event and I attended the funeral in California. Later, I was asked to speak at a Maryland Republican Lincoln Day Dinner on May 4, 1994. The following are my remarks.

Good Evening. As I was at the Nixon funeral last week and as a former Nixon employee, I have been asked to give you some of my impressions and remembrances.

I saw Bill Brock (Republican Senatorial candidate) and Congresswoman Helen Bentley [both in attendance at the dinner] and I am sure they both agree with me that the funeral itself was a most moving and impressive public ceremony. When Senator Dole broke down, we all broke down and tears were on my cheeks as well. But that was as it should be and was expected as, for the most part, we were Nixon loyalists. Men of public life engender deep emotional feelings and Nixon, as with Kennedy and Roosevelt, created extremes. They were polarizing and I don't mean that in a pejorative sense. One was either a strong supporter or opponent, for them or against them — there was no neutrality.

...The element that I found most impressive of all was the reaction of the public, the common man or "the silent majority," as Nixon liked to call them.

The weather was terrible. In life Nixon, the quintessential politician, would have been worried, for dank and rainy weather is detrimental to crowd or rally building. At a funeral, however, the cold and the wind and the low scudding clouds seemed appropriate and the crowds were among the largest he ever drew. People stood in a line that at times stretched up to four miles, winding through the streets of Yorba Linda, all night long in an eight-hour wait. At midnight the local newscasters and police were begging people to stay at home, telling them that there was no chance of getting to walk by the casket, but still they kept coming. When the doors were closed at 11:00 in the morning, some 45,000 people had filed past. They carried signs and they carried little gifts, but most of all they carried flowers. The chamber, of course, could hold only the official arrangements and not even all of them, and so the bouquets accumulated outside until there were thousands of them, on the walks, on the walls, on the lawns...everywhere.

Nixon was the dominant figure in American politics for 25 years and arguably was a dominant world statesman during the same period. His campaign record: two congressional races, one senatorial, two vice presidential, a gubernatorial and three presidential, has never been equaled. In all likelihood this achievement, nine races with seven victories, four of them national, will stand forever as an American record. He was on the cover of *Time Magazine* 56 times, *Newsweek* 54. Nobody else even comes close.

There were some 1500 guests at the ceremony and most of these were in some official capacity. It was the most important funeral since John F. Kennedy's ... in a sense sort of like the Academy awards. It was to Nixon's credit that he was very loyal to his staff. There were invitations to some 100 or so of us who had left our other jobs in 1968 to work for Richard Nixon and then went on to positions in the White House or elsewhere in the administration. We considered ourselves family and the funeral was more than a time of mourning. It was a reunion and a time for contemplation, recognition and celebration of his life and accomplishments. But most of all it was a time for memories.

In that regard, I have one story to share with you which will give you some insight into why I feel Nixon was special.

I was an advance man in the 1968 campaign... It was the toughest job I've ever had. My first assignment was in Houston, Texas, and I was spectacularly lucky. I organized a night rally that drew 50,000 people and [won me] Nixon's appreciation. He sent for me the next morning and told me it was the largest nighttime political event he had ever seen. And from then on, I was golden. More importantly, I continued to be lucky and success followed success. 15,000 people in a suburban Cleveland shopping center on a Saturday morning. In Atlanta, one of the two ticker tape parades of the campaign, the largest crowd ever in Boise. I was the mission impossible advance man. And then I got an impossible mission.

The Midwest is important Republican country and Ohio is key. You cannot become a Republican President without winning Ohio. The schedule for the end of the campaign called for a Midwest swing culminating with a big nighttime rally in Cleveland and then back to New York for a huge blowout at Madison Square Garden on election eve. The polls had us neck and neck with [Hubert] Humphrey, too close to call, and it was critical that the last two events be barnburners. I was sent back to Cleveland, the scene of my previous triumph.

The rally was to be held in downtown Cleveland in the Municipal Auditorium, a cavernous hall seating 10,000.

I pulled out all the stops. I set up a telephone boiler shop with 80 volunteers to drum up business. I spent outrageous sums on radio and newspaper advertising. I got 5,000 balloons filled with helium for a balloon rise. I had another 5,000 balloons suspended from the ceiling for a balloon drop. I got high school kids and Young Republicans and stuffed them with pizza and cokes and got 5,000 hand-painted signs, one for every other seat and an 800 foot long banner wrapped around the inside of the hall. I hired a band. I got 5,000 Styrofoam skimmer hats to go with the signs. I got a ton of confetti and when the fire marshal wouldn't allow it because it wasn't fireproof, I got it repackaged and labeled "ACME fireproof confetti." I got noisemakers. I printed 20,000 tickets and spread them around. And finally, I flew in a load of color-corrected klieg lights so that the television networks could film the triumphant entry of Nixon as he marched down the aisle, from the rear of the hall to the stage.

And I got problems.

I was at the hotel about a half an hour before the motorcade was to load and I got a call on my radio from my assistant at the hall. It was an unmitigated disaster, he explained (although that was not his choice of words). Only 3,000 people had arrived and the press was having a field day. Camera crews were roaming up and down the aisles and photographing the signs and the hats and the empty seats. They were loving it and the pundits were talking about how Nixon had peaked too early, and that this was a sign...

Nixon had to be told, and I was terrified; so I told John Ehrlichman, and *he* told Nixon. Nixon promptly sent for me. "What did you do?" he asked, and I recounted all of my efforts. When I had finished, the next President of the United States (although we certainly didn't know that at the time) looked at me and said: "It's my fault. Don't worry. This is the fifth time I've been to Cleveland and it was too much."

Well, after we had a chance to analyze it we realized there was more to the story. 1968 was the year of the riots, and Cleveland had a huge one in the Hough district, with much burning and looting right downtown close to the auditorium. Further, George Wallace, the third presidential candidate, had held a rally at the same auditorium just ten days earlier and there had been an ugly demonstration with people injured. No force on earth could have persuaded the nice suburban Republicans to come into downtown Cleveland that night.

Nixon went on with the show. The only change was that he walked on from a wing instead of coming down the aisle.

Instead of staying behind to help wrap up the details, as was customary, I was invited to ride back to New York on the Nixon's aircraft. Mrs. Nixon sat with me and tried to be consoling. I appreciated it, but it didn't help. Bob Finch, the former Lieutenant Governor of California and future Secretary of Health Education and Welfare, sat with me and told me the story of how, in 1952, he had taken Nixon to a rally on the wrong night. That didn't help, either. And then Bob Haldeman, an almost mystical figure, sat with me and said, "Tell me about yourself. We are going to need people like you on the White House staff." That helped.

There are three observations to be made: that Nixon was a large enough man to accept the blame; that he was concerned about even junior members of his staff; and that he never, never, never quit or got discouraged, even in the face of a disaster.

This is also an epilogue. At the funeral, David Eisenhower told me that he and Julie were writing a book about the campaign of 1968. Suddenly, his face brightened and he got that Eisenhower smile, and then he said: "Hey, I need to talk to you about Cleveland."

I am often asked why I got involved in politics in the first place. I took four years out of my professional career at a very important time. Politics is frequently a dirty business; people get hurt and many politicians are venal and self-serving. The answer is simple. I thought then, and think to this day, that I was doing something for my country and I consider myself fortunate to have had that opportunity with Richard Nixon.

Thank you.

Epilogue

Following the election in 1972, John Ehrlichman recommended Ed Morgan for a position as Assistant Secretary of the Treasury. Ehrlichman did this in recognition of Morgan's diligent work on the Welfare Reform program. After the Senate confirmed him for that post, we spent some time together. He was happier than I think I had ever seen him. Unfortunately, it was not to last. He became ensnarled in Watergate.

The following article from the December 20, 1974 *Washington Post*, relates the story:

EX NIXON AIDE GETS FOUR MONTHS IN JAIL IN BACKDATING OF '70 DOCUMENTS GIFT

Edward L. Morgan, the attorney who illegally backdated the former President Nixon's 1970 gift of public papers to the Government, was sentenced yesterday to four months in prison.

US District Judge George J. Hart called the sentencing the most difficult task he had performed in his 17 years on the bench, saying that "Morgan was a man whose circumstances cry out for mercy and leniency."

Hart said the attorney was "universally admired" but made "one terrible mistake in an effort to serve with misplaced loyalty a superior who served in the highest office in this land."

However, Hart added Morgan was also an attorney who on that occasion "willfully betrayed his trust to the law and to the public" and "such an action cannot depart this court unflogged."

Morgan pleaded guilty last month to one count of conspiracy to impede, defeat, and obstruct the lawful functions of the Internal Revenue Service by backdating the

183

Nixon deed. No one else has been charged in that conspiracy and the Watergate special prosecutor's office said the investigation is continuing.

President Ford has already pardoned Nixon for any crimes committed while he was in office so he could not be prosecuted.

Morgan told Hart before the sentencing, "I did something I should not have done and it was wrong. I'm prepared to accept the judgment of the court."

His attorney, Richard van Dusen, said that Morgan signed the deed, "knowing that, if he refused to do so, at a minimum...the President might be exposed to great public embarrassment."

Morgan was a White House aide in the spring of 1970 when he was asked to sign a deed dated 1969 in connection with a Nixon gift of vice presidential papers the previous year, according to information filed by prosecutors and interviews with others familiar with the case.

Morgan at first refused, according to sources familiar with the case, but later agreed.

The backdating allowed the Nixons to claim $95,000 as the first installment of a planned $576,000 deduction for a gift of his vice presidential papers.

Last year the Internal Revenue Service ruled against the deduction for the papers, and ordered the Nixons to pay nearly $500,000 in back taxes.

Morgan, who later became an assistant secretary of the Treasury in the Nixon administration, could have been sentenced to five years in jail and fined $10,000 for his plea on the one felony count.

Prosecutors did not ask for a specific sentence for Morgan, but took the unusual step of pointing out to the judge that Morgan had attempted to cover up his crime for several months "by a series of premeditated acts," before deciding to enter his plea and admit his guilt.

Hart imposed a two-year sentence on Morgan, but then said only four months of that time would actually have to be spent in jail. Morgan will be on probation for the remaining 20 months.

Hart gave Morgan until January 6 at 1 p.m. to report to a federal prison at Lompoc, Calif.

Ed came to Rose Hill Farm, our home in Maryland, to spend with us his last three days as a free man. From there, he left to go to prison (which he called "camp"). Together in my pick-up truck, we made the weekly trash run to the county dump. Ed remarked that he was "happy to be my assistant on the dump run, as it might prove to be valuable training for his job after 'camp,' as [he] would not be able to practice law." When we said our good byes, with hugging and backslapping, I had no idea that it was to be the last time I would see him.

While Ed was in prison, I corresponded with him regularly. He kept up his humor and good will.

Jan. 27th

My Dear Stuart,

I have just gazed down from my tiny window into the square where the last public hanging 'till the morrow has been concluded. The Sheriff of Nottingham seemed a bit more paunchy than usual and Maid Marion was not to be seen. It's an usually cold night which makes it all the worse for the poor dogs in the pillories, but such is life.

Please excuse the print on this paper. My friend Gutenberg in the next cell has fashioned blocks of wood with shavings of metal for the type and we must mix salt, crushed black daisies and the blood of a dead rabbit for ink. Thus, writing to you is a slow and laborious process. We have been at this letter a month now.

Six of my colleagues escaped last night, but alas, poor lads, three were caught by the local constable within the hour. Tomorrow we are holding new elections for the escape committee.

Other than that, I'm down to 87 days and doing fine. The time drags on like a bitch but there are some very interesting chaps here, each a character in his own right, including Juan Corona's defense counsel, in on a tax rap, who's a hell of a guy.

Almost a month now, you can imagine I am already counting the days 'til Spring, but you have to take them one at a time. Alma has come up each weekend, along with my brother and some other friends intermittently and that's been a great help — makes each succeeding week doable.

However, I still have my calendar (an old piece of gray slate naturally, written upon with a sharp stone) marked for your generous offer of R & R come May.

On the plus side, I have lost about 15 pounds so far, have joined the conditioning class, and am in the Intermediate tennis class.

Frankly, you sort of go at it as 16 weeks of basic training with no weekend pass, although in many respects there was more hassle in the service. Other things, of course, are not as good as the service, but then you in society do not intend for life to be made easy for we hardened criminals who are a menace to your way of life.

Your training at the trash dump was in vain. I was assigned to the furniture factory because of my outstanding aptitude in working with my hands.

I began working as a Sander 4th class in the sanding room (a delightful spa if you enjoy breathing dust by the bushel basket) wherein I ruined 5 bookshelves my first day. After but a scant two weeks there (most are moved out within 3 days) I was laterally arabesqued to Power Saw Operator 4th class where I lift and cut lumber all day. Now, provided I don't saw my nuts off, or some equally treasured appendage, I'll be O.K.

By the way, any worries I had about money were for naught. I earn 27 cents an hour at the factory so am planning an early retirement.

Trust things are going well for you and Connie. Look forward to sharing some accumulated stories in the Spring.

More anon.

Thanks, most sincerely again, for everything.

Ed (or 1177, for short)

And another.

Feb. 19

Dear Bonnie & Clyde,

Thanks for your great letter, and I'm glad to hear they haven't caught up with you yet. I think you're smart to settle in the East like you have and stay the hell out of Kansas. And buying a farm is a great idea. Talk about plenty of room to bury the swack!

Speaking of that, I hate to raise a delicate issue but your letter indicates my share, which you've properly placed in tin cans and buried in your garden, comes to $848,766.45. A thorough review of my records reveals the figure should be $848,767.95

I suggest that the error could result from your failure to take into account the following:

$.20 I loaned you for phone call to your Mother just before the Jones Bank job.

$.70 Cab fare for Bonnie to meet us at the Inverness Bridge for the Brinks stickup

$.35 Burger I bought Clyde during the getaway from Topeka Post Office job.

$.15 Coke I bought Bonnie while waiting to knock off the Union Pacific at Grady's Crossing.

$.10 Cost of bullet I loaned Clyde to shoot the bank dick in Kansas City.

$1.50

I certainly trust you won't consider this quibbling on my part, but I've believed that these matters should be dealt with openly between partners. Just like the time Knuckles Rattigan said you owed him a quarter for a pay toilet stop and you machine gunned him down right there in the ice cream parlor in front of the Sunday School class.

On second thought, forget it.

Life here goes on at its same mad cap pace. I did bump into the Count of Monte Cristo in the yard the other day and remembered you to him. He's not very talkative to us short-timers.

Sorry to hear Rio was a disappointment. However, it does mean that you are my first friend who can finally answer that musical question of the '40s for me, "What do they do on a rainy night in Rio?" (posed by the Andrews sisters, if I'm not mistaken).

My scheduled release date should beat the Kentucky Derby. It's currently set for 6:A.M., April 23rd. Thus, this weekend means it's half over and downhill from here. And it seems like only ten years ago that I arrived.

You can be proud that my storehouse of knowledge continues to grow. No longer do I saw or sand, I now work the 4 P.M. to midnight shift at the power-house. So, if nothing else, you can be thankful you live on the East coast and not in this immediate vicinity. I'll let you know what it is I do there just as soon as I figure it out.

Keep 'em flying. Spring is just around the corner.

And then, this classic Ed Morgan:

AN AUTHENTIC "GET WELL"

MESSAGE FROM PRISON

Hey, Bro —

What's happenin', man? Was cruising the freeway when my crimee says they capped on ya and you're all timed out. Who hung a jacket on ya, man. Don't let 'em get on your case.

Sounds like a bad beef with finger waves and X-rays. So my main man, don't get yim-yammed or okey-doked, you hear? Play it to the max. I'll hit the ramp and jigger soon as I'm off front street. Then we can break it out and be havin' things. No more donkey dicks and Polish genasco, you know? Guacamole from the gate.

Esse' you in the flats or where? They up in your face? Don't go coppin' deuces 'cause it ain't nothin' but a meatball and they can't eat you. Square biz, runnin' part-ner, get it on. You snooze, you lose. Far out!

Vault your keyster stash, low rider, and we'll break out the clavo when I drive up. Zuzus and wham-whams and get it all together! You know it ain't 'till the wheels fall off.

Kick back and stay mellow, its gonna be bonarue. I'll be bogartin' my path East after those A.M.s and P.M.s, pal, cause I ain't bowlegged or runnin' wild.

Kite you later.

1177

After he was released, we continued to exchange letters and phone calls for a year or so. I obtained an interview for Ed with the Chairman of my company, who was seeking someone to manage the legal affairs of our corporation and function as an in-house legal advisor. However, the job was in Puerto Rico and Morgan did not want to leave California. He took a position managing an apartment house in order to get free housing. He tried to get into the movies as a script-writer, an effort in which he was unsuccessful.

Then, without warning, he dropped off the face of the earth. His phone was disconnected. His letters were returned, with no forwarding address. I heard nothing for more than 20 years and began to fear that he was dead. Clearly, he did not wish to see anybody from his past. I believe he did this because he perceived himself a failure in life. It may also have been that he had created a new life for himself and did not wish to be reminded of the old one. Perhaps it was a little of both.

In 1999, as the following letter relates, I obtained his address and wrote him:

15 March 99

Dear Ed:

After John's Ehrlichman's death several weeks ago, I was musing in my office about him and the times we had together. As I was at my computer, I went "online" and searched for Egil Krogh (how many of *them* could there be)? I called him in Seattle and really surprised him. In the course of our conversation I asked him if he knew where you were; hence this letter.

I do not know where to begin...what does one say after a gap of more than 20 years? I'll begin by trying to fill in the important events in my life:

I am now recovering from my third brain tumor operation. You were in "camp" at the time of the first, and I had a fairly rough time with this one. When I awoke from the anesthesia I was paralyzed on the right side and could not move my arm or leg more than a few inches. To shorten a long story, I had physical therapy, occupational therapy and speech pathology therapy through the Fall and am now about 90% recovered. If you recall the thrill you felt when, as a small boy you tied your shoes for the first time, I can certify the rapture is no less the second time around. The *ne plus ultra*, however, is being bathroom independent.

I left IGC nearly five years ago after a serious policy disagreement with Jim Wilson, started my own business and have been, to put it frankly, struggling ever since. Being a land developer today has less panache than being an attorney and it takes forever to get a project approved. As the first part of the decade was also rough, I do not look back on the 90s with any fondness.

We are still at Rose Hill and now grow vegetables and sell them from a country store, which I built. Connie runs the farm and won't let me interfere, except to participate in manual labor from time to time. I regret to inform you that we now have a trash dumpster on the farm so your job as Assistant Waste Disposal Officer, a position I held open for many years, is no longer available.

Ed, I am delighted you have decided to "surface" again. Your friends, of which there are many, have long been worried about you. Although I rarely see anyone from the Nixon years, whenever I encountered anyone from that experience, I asked about you and your whereabouts. I always received the same reply, until last week with Bud. Welcome back!

Your old buddy,

Nine months later, I received the following letter from his lady friend:

Dear Charles,

I was going through Ed Morgan's papers the other day and came across your letter and decided to drop you a line. Ed had started to answer your letter but had only written a couple of lines before putting it down and never got around to finishing it.

I don't know if you are aware that Ed died on August 6th from complications from leukemia. He had been diagnosed with leukemia and diabetes in 1995 and was in and out of the hospital for the next four years. He collapsed at home in June of this year and was rushed into the intensive care unit where he seemed to make a pretty good recovery and the doctors were optimistic that he would return home. On August 3rd, he was returned to a medical ward where they were hopeful that he might soon be strong enough to start physical therapy. He seemed to be doing okay when I left the hospital that night but in the early hours of the morning he went into what they call a "blast crisis" and a crisis team intervened to save his life. When I dashed back to the hospital he was on artificial life support and the doctors told me that nothing further could be done except make him comfortable.

189

On a happier note, Ed was delighted to receive your letter and he fully intended to answer it at some point when he was strong enough. He said you were a great guy and said that you were one of those people who were good at whatever you turned your hand to.

***

In the military, there are two toasts traditionally offered at "Dinings In," or other gatherings of old soldiers. The first is: *To the President of the United States.* The other: *To absent friends.*